COMMON STOCKS
AND
COMMON SENSE

COMMON STOCKS

AND

COMMON SENSE

The Strategies, Analyses, Decisions,
and Emotions of a Particularly
Successful Value Investor

Edgar Wachenheim III

WILEY

Published by John Wiley & Sons, Inc., Hoboken, New Jersey.
Published simultaneously in Canada.

For general information on our other products and services or for technical support, please contact our Customer Care Department within the United States at (800) 762-2974, outside the United States at (317) 572-3993 or fax (317) 572-4002.

Wiley publishes in a variety of print and electronic formats and by print-on-demand. Some material included with standard print versions of this book may not be included in e-books or in print-on-demand. If this book refers to media such as a CD or DVD that is not included in the version you purchased, you may download this material at http://booksupport.wiley.com. For more information about Wiley products, visit www.wiley.com.

Library of Congress Cataloging-in-Publication Data:

ISBN 9781119259602 (Hardcover)
ISBN 9781119259626 (ePDF)
ISBN 9781119259930 (ePub)

Printed in the United States of America

10 9 8 7 6 5 4 3 2 1

To my loving wife, Sue, my four children,
and my six grandchildren.
After health, nothing is more important than family.

The author will donate all royalties received from sales of this book to a
charitable foundation.

CONTENTS

INTRODUCTION

I have a passion for common stocks. For the past 30-plus years, I have studied the fundamentals of companies and industries, interviewed managements, visited offices and factories, constructed models of possible future earnings, and made thousands of decisions to purchase and sell stocks. My endeavors have been intense, exciting, fun, and successful. Thousands of other investment managers, many with higher IQs than mine, also have intensively searched for stocks that will appreciate sharply, but relatively few have been as successful as I have been. Why have I been able to succeed? There is no simple answer. If there were a simple answer, most others also would have found and adopted successful approaches to investing and would have enjoyed outsized returns. This has not happened. However, there must be reasons why some investors are better than others.

With the hope that others will benefit from my approach to investing, this book will explore what I believe to be the reasons for my relative success and will describe the reasoning behind the investment decisions that I made over the years. How will I do this? I am a product of the Harvard Business School, which teaches business via the case method. Because I believe that the case method is an interesting, relevant, and effective way to explain the strategies and thinking behind business and investment decisions, I used the method in this book. Chapters 3 through 13 in this book give an inside view of 11 investments made over the years by Greenhaven Associates, the investment management firm I founded in 1987. The explanations summarize Greenhaven's actual investment process: our research, our analysis, our models, and our decisions. The explanations also try to explain the behavioral sides of being in the investment business: our emotions, aspirations, hopes, elations, disappointments. These chapters are the meat of the book and should give the reader a detailed inside view of how an investment manager spends his time and makes his decisions. Also, and importantly, the chapters should give the reader a material understanding of why I have been a successful investor—of what has worked and not worked.

In order to give the reader a better understanding of the investment decisions made in Chapters 3 through 13, I have included Chapter 1, which explains Greenhaven's basic approaches and strategies to investing. And because an investor's success in carrying out his strategies is heavily dependent on his personality, temperament, and lifetime experiences, I have included Chapter 2 about my innate abilities and, more important, about my personality, emotions, and educational and professional experiences.

Chapter 14, the final chapter of this book, is a letter I wrote to Jack Elgart, a younger investor who asked for advice on becoming a successful investment manager. This chapter summarizes my investment strategies and lists a number of "do's and don'ts" that I found useful over the years.

When I was in my teens and 20s, my father continually advised me that it is a gift to hide one's abilities—and my father-in-law continually counseled that one should not call attention to oneself. Why, then, did I write this book? Why the disobedience to elders whom I respected and loved? Here is why. Investing in common stocks has been my life's work, my passion, my fun, my source of income, my source of wealth. Over the years, with hopes of becoming a better investor, I have studied hard and thought intensively about why some investment ideas have worked for me and why others have not. And I have thought about the innate abilities, experiences, creativity, and mental states of those who became successful investors, and about those who did not. As a result of these efforts, I developed the psychological and analytical approaches to investing that have been successful for me. In recent years, I developed a strong desire—almost a calling—to share these approaches and experiences with others lest they be lost to time. That is why I wrote this book.

While the basic facts behind each of the described investments in this book are accurate, I have forgotten many of the details, such as exact conversations, estimates of revenues and earnings, dates, and locations. These I approximated wherever possible—or, in some cases, pulled from my imperfect memory. In addition, I have taken the liberty of changing the names and backgrounds of some individuals in order to protect their privacy. I have also revised the original letter to Jack Elgart to include additional approaches and strategies and to expand some explanations.

I strongly hope that this book stimulates thought about the investment process. Even if the reader does not agree with parts or all of my approach to investing, if the book motivates the reader to think deeply about the science and art of investing, I will feel that the time and effort devoted to writing this book were time and effort well spent.

1

MY APPROACH TO INVESTING

Note: Most of the contents of this chapter will not be new to the majority of experienced investors. I wrote this chapter to bring less experienced investors up to speed with the principles of value investing.

In my opinion, good investing largely is common sense, made somewhat difficult by the behavioral imperfections of man. We can start with the straightforward concept that, over the longer term, common stocks are an unusually attractive investment vehicle, even for an investor whose returns only equal the stock market's returns. During the 50-year period 1960 through 2009, the average U.S. common stock provided an average annual total return (capital gains plus dividends) of 9 to 10 percent. In addition to providing this favorable return, common stocks are highly marketable and therefore can be purchased and sold easily without high frictional costs. Also, and importantly, if selected properly, common stocks offer considerable protection against risks of permanent loss. What could be better: favorable returns, high liquidity, and relative safety! That is a home-run combination, and that is why I am a great fan of common stocks.

The 9 to 10 percent average annual return provided by common stocks over the 50-year period makes economic sense. During the period, if adjustments are made for a few outlier years,[1] the U.S. economy grew at roughly a 6 percent annual rate: about 3 percent from real growth (unit output) and about 3 percent from inflation (increases in prices). Corporate revenues during the period increased in line with the economy, and corporate earnings roughly increased in line with revenues. While the price-to-earnings (PE) ratios of U.S. common stocks have fluctuated widely during the 50-year period, they seem to fluctuate around an average of about 16 times earnings. Therefore, before consideration of corporate acquisitions and share repurchases, common stocks have appreciated at about a 6 percent average annual rate over the years due to the growth of the economy.

U.S. corporations, on average, generate considerably more cash than they require to support their growth. This excess cash can be used by corporations to pay dividends, acquire other companies, or repurchase their own shares. Over the past 50 years, dividends have provided a 2.5+ percent yield, and acquisitions and share repurchases together have increased the earnings per share (EPS) growth of publicly traded corporations by close to 1 percent per year.

Thus, an average company's EPS has grown at about a 6 percent rate "organically" and at about a 7 percent rate including acquisitions and share repurchases. If one then adds the 2.5+ percent dividend yield to this 7 percent, the result is the 9 to 10 percent total return that an average investor has received over the years from investing in common stocks.

While it is difficult to project the future, assuming that the United States continues to be reasonably prosperous and capitalistic, I see no reason why the U.S. stock market will not continue to provide average annual returns of 9 to 10 percent over the longer run, even if the U.S. economy grows at a somewhat slower pace than it has in the past. If future growth is somewhat dampened, then corporations will not need to reinvest as much of their cash flows back into their businesses to support growth. Therefore, corporations should have more free cash available to pay dividends, acquire other companies, or repurchase their shares—and the increased returns from these uses of cash should mostly or completely offset the reduced returns from the slower growth.

In spite of the many positive attributes of common stocks, I believe that many investors shy away from owning common stocks because they are fearful of the stock market's volatility, especially sharp downturns that are accompanied by negative news from the media and from Wall Street. Many consider volatility to be a risk. Importantly, when thinking about risk, I draw a sharp distinction between permanent loss and volatility. The former is what it says it is: a loss that cannot be recovered. Permanent losses are hurtful and should be avoided at all cost—avoided like the black plague. They are decidedly detrimental to the creation of wealth. Volatility, however, is merely stocks or markets going up and down in price (not in value). Downward volatility usually is nerve-racking, but otherwise is quite harmless. Markets and stocks tend to fluctuate. They always have, and they probably always will. Importantly, every time the market has declined, it eventually has fully recovered and then has appreciated to new heights. The financial crisis during the fall of 2008 and the winter of 2009 is an extreme (and outlier) example of volatility. During the six months between the end of August 2008 and end of February 2009, the Standard & Poor's (S&P) 500 Index fell by 42 percent from 1,282.83 to 735.09. Yet by early 2011 the S&P 500 had recovered to the 1,280 level, and by August 2014 it had appreciated to the 2000 level. An investor who purchased the S&P 500 Index on August 31, 2008, and then sold the Index six years later, lived through the worst financial crisis and recession since the Great Depression, but still earned a 56 percent profit on his[2] investment before including dividends—and 69 percent including the dividends that he would have received during the six-year period. Earlier, I mentioned that over a 50-year period, the stock market provided an average annual return of 9 to 10 percent. During the six-year period August 2008 through August 2014, the stock market provided an average annual return of 11.1 percent—above the range of normalcy in spite of the abnormal horrors and consequences of the financial crisis and resulting deep recession.

Thus, it appears that the 2008–2009 financial crisis, as scary as it was, did not have a material long-term effect on the aggregate value of U.S. common stocks. The volatility during the crisis turned out to be inconsequential for the patient long-term investor.

In fact, an investor should treat volatility as a friend. High volatility permits an investor to purchase stocks when they are particularly depressed and to sell the stocks when they are selling at particularly high prices. The greater the volatility, the greater the opportunity to purchase stocks at very low prices and then sell the stocks at very high prices. But what happens when the price of a stock falls sharply after you purchase it? No problem, assuming that the stock was an undervalued investment at the price you paid for it. Eventually, the price of the stock should recover and then appreciate well above your cost basis.

This leads me to another important positive attribute of common stocks. An investor can decide the exact times he wishes to buy and sell a stock, and the only determinants of his success are the cost of the stock at the time of purchase and the price of the stock at the time of sale. While the unfortunate schoolchild's final grade in a subject usually includes his interim grades on homework assignments, class participation, pop quizzes, and interim tests, the only grade that counts for an investor is the profit earned on a stock at the moment the investor decides to sell the stock. An investor might purchase shares of a company at $80. The price of the shares might then decline to $40 (a failing grade) and remain at the $40 level for a full year (definitely a failing grade). Then the shares might start rising, reaching a price of $160 three years after the investor made his purchase (an A+ grade). The investor might then sell the shares at $160, thereby doubling his money in three years. When the investor receives his report card, his final grade is A+. All the interim failing grades have been thrown out. It made no difference that the shares sold at $40 for a one-year period. The interim price was not relevant, unless the investor had been forced to sell the shares when they were at $40. Or unless the investor had the resources and desire to purchase additional shares when they were at $40, in which case the $40 price was a blessing—and the extreme volatility in the price of the shares functioned as a close friend.

While many investors believe that they should continually reduce their risks to a possible decline in the stock market, I disagree. Every time the stock market has declined, it eventually has more than fully recovered. Hedging the stock market by shorting stocks, or by buying puts on the S&P 500 Index, or by any other method usually is expensive and, in the long run, is a waste of money. But how do you protect yourself if the stock market temporarily increases to excessively high levels, as it does from time to time? Then, it is likely that individual stocks in your portfolio will be sold because their prices will have increased to levels where their risk-to-reward ratios have become unattractive, and it is also likely that the level of cash held in your portfolio will increase (maybe to a very large percentage of the portfolio) because it will be difficult to find attractive new ideas in an inflated market. The cash then provides protection from a decline in the market. However, and importantly, the buildup of the cash is not a conscious effort to provide protection against a decline in an excessively priced market, but rather is a result of the height of the market.

Thus, common-stock investors of average ability should be able to earn 9 to 10 percent average annual returns without taking large risks of permanent loss. I have a thesis to explain the particularly favorable reward-to-risk attractiveness of common stocks. The return investors demand from any type of investment is a function of the perceived risk of the investment. The higher the perceived risk, the higher the demanded return. As discussed earlier, most investors incorrectly consider volatility to be a risk. These investors thus demand a higher return from common stocks than the deserved return. This error is our opportunity—and is another reason we treat volatility as a friend.

While the stock market itself is attractive, my goal, hope, and prayers are to materially outperform the stock market over time. My specific objective is to achieve average annual returns of 15 to 20 percent without subjecting our portfolios to large risks of permanent loss. Happily, we have achieved these goals. Over the past 25 years, accounts that we manage have achieved average annual returns of very close to 19 percent. I attribute a material part of this success to a strategy that I developed in the early 1980s. The strategy is to try to purchase deeply undervalued securities of strong and growing companies that hopefully will appreciate sharply as the result of positive developments that already have not been largely discounted into the prices of the securities. Our reasoning is that the undervaluation, growth, and strength should provide the protection we cherish against permanent loss, while the undervaluation, strength, growth, and positive developments should present the opportunity to earn high returns. We typically purchase shares in a company in anticipation that one or more positive developments will drive the shares within the next few years, and we then sell the shares after the positive development (or developments) has occurred and has been substantially discounted into the price of the shares. Positive developments can include a cyclical upturn in an industry, the development of an exciting new product or service, the sale of a company to another company, the replacement of a poor management with a good one, the initiation of a major cost reduction program, or the initiation of a major share repurchase program. Importantly, the positive developments we predict should not already have been predicted by a large number of other investors. We need to be creative and well ahead of the curve. If we are not early, there is a likelihood that the future positive developments already largely will have been discounted into the price of the shares.

But what if we are wrong about a stock and the predicted positive development fails to occur (which does happen)? Then, the undervaluation, strength, and growth of the stock still provide the opportunity to earn a reasonable return. If we cannot have the icing, we can at least have the cake.

The above strategy of predicting positive changes makes common sense. At any one time, the price of a stock reflects the weighted opinion of the majority of investors. In order to earn outsized returns, we need to hold opinions about the future that are different and more accurate than those of the majority of other investors. In fact, it can be said that successful investing is all about predicting the future more accurately than the majority of other investors.

Previously, I stated that common stocks, if selected properly, offer considerable protection against the risks of permanent loss. But what criteria do we use to select stocks that offer that protection? Of course, there are no formulas for analyzing the risks of permanent loss. It is said that if investing could be reduced to formulas, the richest people in the world all would be mathematicians. However, there are several signs to look for. A company that has a leveraged balance sheet (large quantities of debt relative to its cash flows and assets) may not have sufficient cash during difficult times to pay the interest it owes on its debt, in which case it might have to file for bankruptcy (in bankruptcy proceedings, the common shareholder usually loses most of his investment). A company whose value is dependent on a single technology might permanently lose most of its value if the technology becomes obsolete. For example, digital cameras have obsoleted Kodak's chemical-based films, with the result that Kodak has permanently lost most of its value. An investor also can suffer a permanent loss if he pays far too high a price for a stock.

To help minimize the risks of permanent loss, I look for a margin of safety in the stocks that we purchase. The concept of a margin of safety is that an investor should purchase a security at a price sufficiently below his estimate of its intrinsic value that he will have protection against permanent loss even if his estimate proves somewhat optimistic. An analogy is an investor standing on the 10th floor of a building, waiting for an elevator to carry him to the lobby. The elevator door opens. The investor notices that the elevator is rated for 600 pounds. There already are two relatively obese men in the elevator. The investor estimates their weights at about 200 pounds each. The investor knows that he weighs 175 pounds. The investor should not enter the elevator. There is an inadequate margin of safety. Maybe he underestimated the weights of the two obese men. Maybe the elevator company overestimated the strength of the elevator's cable. The investor waits for the next elevator. The door opens. There is one skinny old lady in the elevator. The investor says hello to the lady and enters the elevator. On his ride to the lobby, he will enjoy a large margin of safety.

I note that our quest for a margin of safety makes us "value" investors as opposed to "growth stock" investors. As a value investor, we pay great attention to the price we pay for a security relative to our estimate of its intrinsic value. However, a growth stock investor pays considerable attention to the growth rate of a company and less attention to the price he pays for the growth. If a growth-stock investor purchases shares in a company that is growing at a 15 percent rate and if he holds the shares for many years, most of his returns will come from the growth as opposed to any change in the share's price-to-earnings (PE) ratio. Therefore, most growth investors are willing to pay a high PE ratio for a security. I have a problem with growth-stock investing. Companies tend not to grow at high rates forever. Businesses change with time. Markets mature. Competition can increase. Good managements can retire and be replaced with poor ones. Indeed, the stock market is littered with once highly profitable growth stocks that have become less profitable cyclic stocks as a result of losing their competitive edge. Kodak is one example. Xerox is another. IBM is a third. And there are hundreds of others. When growth stocks permanently falter, the price of their shares can fall sharply as their PE ratios contract and, sometimes, as their earnings fall—and investors in the shares can suffer serious permanent loss. Many investors claim that they will be able to sell the shares of a faltering growth stock before the price of the shares declines sharply, but, in practice, it is difficult to determine whether a company is facing a temporary threat that it will overcome or whether it is facing a permanent adverse change. And when it becomes apparent to an audience that there is a fire in a theater, only a small fraction of the audience can be among the first to flee through an exit door. Therefore, many growth-stock investors do suffer permanent losses.

In addition to shying away from paying high multiples for growth stocks, I tend to avoid the shares of weaker companies, even if their shares are selling at distressed prices. Some value investors are attracted to the deeply depressed shares of poorly positioned companies that have uncertain futures. I call these "cigar butt" investments. They are good for a few more puffs, but that is all. I strongly prefer purchasing undervalued shares of strong and well-positioned companies. My experience is that it sometimes takes a number of years for the prices of undervalued shares to increase to their intrinsic values or to be buoyed by positive events. During the time an investor owns a poorly positioned company, its intrinsic value might increase slowly, or, in some cases, might even decline to the level where the investor faces a permanent loss. However, the intrinsic value of a well-positioned company should increase in excess of 7 percent per year.[3] This is why we say that time is a friend of a good business and an enemy of a poor business.

Investors often are faced with the choice of purchasing a riskier stock with particularly large upside potential or a much less risky stock with less upside potential. Our proclivity is to purchase the less risky stock because we are great believers in Warren Buffett's two rules to being a successful investor. The first rule is to avoid serious permanent loss, and the second rule is to never forget the first rule. There are good reasons for this emphasis on risk avoidance. If an investor sells one stock at a 50 percent loss and reinvests the proceeds in a second stock, the second stock would have to appreciate by 100 percent before the investor recovers his loss in the first stock. Furthermore, large permanent losses can dampen the confidence of an investor—and I strongly believe that a good investor needs to be highly confident about his ability to make decisions, because investment decisions seldom are clear and usually are muddled with uncertainties and unknowns.

Our strategies of being risk averse (but being indifferent to volatility) and of purchasing undervalued stocks of strong and growing companies that hopefully will appreciate sharply as a result of positive changes are important reasons for our success over the years. But most other investors, including many who are highly intelligent and experienced, also have sensible investment strategies and yet are unable to materially outperform the S&P 500 Index. Why? My strong answer—and a key point in this book—is that a successful investor also needs certain other abilities that are more behavioral than analytical. In particular, I believe that a successful investor must be adept at making contrarian decisions that are counter to the conventional wisdom, must be confident enough to reach conclusions based on probabilistic future developments as opposed to extrapolations of recent trends, and must be able to control his emotions during periods of stress and difficulties. These three behavioral attributes are so important that they merit further analysis.

BEING A CONTRARIAN

Because at any one time the price of a stock is determined by the opinion of the majority of investors, a stock that appears undervalued to us appears appropriately valued to most other investors. Therefore, by taking the position that the stock is undervalued, we are taking a contrarian position—a position that is unpopular and often is very lonely. Our experience is that while many investors claim they are contrarians, in practice most find it difficult to buck the conventional wisdom and invest counter to the prevailing opinions and sentiments of other investors, Wall Street analysts, and the media. Most individuals and most investors simply end up being followers, not leaders.

In fact, I believe that the inability of most individuals to invest counter to prevailing sentiments is habitual and, most likely, a genetic trait. I cannot prove this scientifically, but I have witnessed many intelligent and experienced investors who shunned undervalued stocks that were under clouds, favored fully valued stocks that were in vogue, and repeated this pattern year after year even though it must have become apparent to them that the pattern led to mediocre results at best. One such example is a gentleman with whom I periodically dine to discuss investment ideas. I will call him Danny Dinner Date. Danny has a high IQ and has been in the investment business for more than 40 years. He graduated near the top of his class from a rigorous private high school and attended an Ivy League college. He worked for many years as a securities analyst and portfolio manager, and eventually headed up a sizable investment management company. Danny's resume is A+. Yet Danny's investment results are only mediocre—maybe C or C+. Danny will listen intently when I describe an undeservedly depressed stock that likely should appreciate sharply in response to the expected easing of a temporary problem, and he frequently will appear interested in purchasing the stock. However, in follow-up conversations, Danny often will mention that he is waiting for some signal that the problem has eased before purchasing the stock. Of course, by the time such a signal becomes apparent to Danny Dinner Date, it is likely that the easing already has become apparent to many other investors and that the price of the shares already has discounted part or all of the forthcoming change. Danny, therefore, is prone to purchasing stocks that already have appreciated sharply. Because Danny is fully aware of his mistimings, I readily conclude that his inability to purchase stocks that are under a cloud is habitual. He simply lacks the ability to be a contrarian leader and instead becomes a follower of the herd.

HAVING CONFIDENCE

Investment decisions seldom are clear. The information an investor receives about the fundamentals of a company usually is incomplete and often is conflicting. Every company has present or potential problems as well as present or future strengths. One cannot be sure about the future demand for a company's products or services, about the success of any new products or services introduced by competitors, about future inflationary cost increases, or about dozens of other relevant variables. So investment outcomes are uncertain. However, when making decisions, an investor often can assess the probabilities of certain outcomes occurring and then make his decisions based on the probabilities. Investing is probabilistic.

In my opinion, reaching rational decisions in a probabilistic world requires confidence. I have observed that investors who lack confidence often delay making decisions in quest of additional information that supports their views. Sometimes the delays become permanent and opportunities are permanently lost. Warren Buffett says that investors do not have

11

to swing at every pitch. But an investor who lets too many good pitches go by because he possesses the confidence to swing only at particularly "fat" pitches may be called out on strikes before he ever sees a particularly fat pitch.

During my career, I purchased many stocks that I should not have and failed to purchase other stocks that I should have. I often have been asked how I can maintain my investment confidence in light of the many decisions that did not turn out as predicted. I have an answer to this question. To maintain my confidence and to guard against decision regret (becoming distraught over opportunities that were missed or over purchases that were unsuccessful), I draw a large distinction between the correctness of my decisions and the outcomes of my decisions. If I carefully analyze a security and if my analysis is based on sufficiently large quantities of accurate information, I always will be making a correct decision. Granted, the outcome of the decision might not be as I had wanted, but I know that decisions always are probabilistic and that subsequent unpredictable changes or events can alter outcomes. Thus, I do my best to make decisions that make sense given everything I know, and I do not worry about the outcomes. An analogy might be my putting game in golf. Before putting, I carefully try to assess the contours and speed of the green. I take a few practice strokes. I aim the putter to the desired line. I then putt and hope for the best. Sometimes the ball goes into the hole, but most often it misses. I do not worry about missing or the misses. By removing worry from the decision-making process in golf and in investing, I can think more rationally and act more confidently—and therefore make better decisions, especially when investment decisions are counter to the conventional wisdom or otherwise are difficult. And I can sleep at night!

CONTROLLING EMOTIONS

I have observed that when the stock market or an individual stock is weak, there is a tendency for many investors to have an emotional response to the poor performance and to lose perspective and patience. The loss of perspective and patience often is reinforced by negative reports from Wall Street and from the media, who tend to overemphasize the significance of the cause of the weakness. We have an expression that airplanes take off and land every day by the tens of thousands, but the only ones you read about in the newspapers are the ones that crash. Bad news sells. To the extent that negative news triggers further selling pressures on stocks and further emotional responses, the negativism tends to feed on itself. Surrounded by negative news, investors tend to make irrational and expensive decisions that are based more on emotions than on fundamentals. This leads to the frequent sales of stocks when the news is bad and vice versa. Of course, the investor usually sells stocks after they already have materially declined in price and usually purchases stocks after they already have materially increased in price. Thus, trading the market based on emotional reactions to short-term news usually is expensive—and sometimes very expensive. John Maynard Keynes said the following about trading the market: "Most of those who attempt it sell too late, buy too late, and do both too often."[4]

On October 19, 1987, the S&P 500 Index declined by 20.9 percent due to panic selling. There were no apparent fundamental reasons for the sharp decline. That evening, the faces of my co-commuters on the train to Rye, New York, were ashen. As I exited the train, I said hello to a friend who managed a medium-sized investment management firm. My friend, who looked most upset, commented that the day's collapse in the market was the worst financial disaster since the Great Depression—that most investors likely would lose confidence in the equity markets, triggering further declines in the prices of stocks, and that it would take years for the markets to recover. My friend said that he had sold some stocks that day and intended to sell more on the following day. I was dismayed by my friend's logic—or, rather, lack of logic. Let us assume that my friend owned stock X on October 18 because he believed it was worth $14 versus its then selling price of $10. Let us further assume that the stock fell in line with the market on October 19 and closed the day at $7.90. My friend now intended to sell the stock at $7.90 even though the day earlier he believed it was worth $14. Such a sale would be nonsensical. My friend had acted on emotion, not on reason. And my friend's mistake was costly. During the next two years, the S&P 500 Index appreciated by more than 50 percent.

Seth Klarman, the founder of the Baupost Group, once said that "people don't consciously choose to invest with emotion—they simply can't help it."[5] Based on my observations, it would be easy for me to agree with Seth Klarman. I have continually seen intelligent and experienced investors repeatedly lose control of their emotions and repeatedly make ill-advised decisions during periods of stress. Surely, these intelligent and experienced investors must realize that their emotions are central to their mistakes. Why haven't they learned from the mistakes and tamed their emotions? Is their inability to think and act unemotionally during periods of stress habitual, ingrained in their personality? I cannot be sure of the answers to these questions, but I am not giving up on the notion that human beings, through effort and thought, can repress their emotions sufficiently to make rational decisions during periods of stress. All it takes is self-discipline—maybe a lot of self-discipline, but not an insurmountable amount for investors who are willing to be challenged. Here is one approach. When an investor is barraged with particularly bad or good news, he can reread the memos, notes, and models he wrote before the occurrence of the news. He then can ask himself three questions: What really has changed? How have the changes affected the value of the investments under consideration? Am I sure that my appraisal of the changes is rational and is not being overly influenced by the immediacy and the severity of the news? By being aware of one's emotions and by consciously trying to control them, investors should be able to make better decisions. This is important because, in my opinion, overreactions to current news are a major cause of underperformance in the stock market.

• • •

I believe that the readers of Chapters 3 through 13 will conclude that my abilities to be a contrarian, to invest with confidence, and to control my emotions are the principal reasons for my success over the years. Yes, the techniques of analysis that most books emphasize are important, but the importance is relevant only if an uncluttered, logical, confident, and unemotional mind has the ability to use the techniques to make successful investment decisions. That is the crux of this book.

Therefore, if an individual believes that he has the behavioral traits, plus the analytical skills and knowledge,[6] to be a successful investor, I recommend that he should go for it and become an active investor who analyzes and owns common stocks. Active investing should work for him and provide above-average returns. And an active investor should enjoy the thrill and the intellectual satisfaction of analyzing, selecting, and owning stocks.

However, if an individual believes that he does not have the ability to become a successful investor, he should invest passively—in index funds or in broadly based exchange-traded funds (ETFs) that are designed to roughly equal the market's performance. The recent proliferation of index funds and ETFs is evidence that many investors have concluded that they cannot outperform the stock market over time. For the sake of our nation, I applaud this trend. Most individuals should not try to compete against talented professional investors any more than most weekend tennis players should try to play matches against world-ranked professional tennis players. They will lose, usually badly.

NOTES

1. Inflation rates during the years 1973 to 1982 were abnormally high.
2. In this book, every time I refer to "his" or "he," I am also referring to "her" or "she."
3. Intrinsic values should increase in line with the growth of EPS. As indicated previously, over the past 50 years, the EPS of an average company has grown at a 7 percent or so annual rate.
4. John Maynard Keynes, "Memorandum for the Estates Committee." Paper presented to the Estates Committee, Kings College at Cambridge University, May 8, 1938.
5. Barton Biggs, *Hedgehogging* (Hoboken, NJ: Wiley, 2008), 259.
6. Access to information can be an important competitive edge for an investor—and, admittedly, professional investors usually have access to more information than nonprofessionals do.

2

THE BRIEF STORY OF
MY LIFE

Because I believe that so much of an investor's success is a function of his personality, I believe that it is useful for a reader of this book to have a substantial understanding of my DNA and my life experiences. If I had been born with a different personality or been mentored by different educators or bosses, my investment styles, decisions, and successes likely would have been quite different from what they are. Therefore, before trying to understand why I made certain investment decisions, I have provided substantial background about me. The background is divided into eight sections.

1. WILLINGNESS AND ABILITY TO BE AN INDEPENDENT THINKER AND A CONTRARIAN

I always have been an independent thinker who is willing and able to make decisions that are counter to the conventional wisdom.

According to my parents, I was an independent thinker at a young age. Evidently, when in first grade, I gave my parents a difficult time by questioning the existence of a myriad of intangibles, including God, Santa

Claus, and the tooth fairy (even though the tooth fairy regularly placed quarters under my pillow whenever I lost a first tooth). I was the consummate Doubting Thomas. In high school, college, and, especially, Harvard Business School, I enjoyed the intellectual process of pioneering positions that were original or that were counter to those of other students and, sometimes, even to those of my teachers.

One example of my contrary and contrarian nature sticks out in my mind. In high school, my American history teacher was Mr. Donald Erickson. Every school day, Mr. Erickson lectured on a particular event in our nation's history and then assigned us to read about the event that evening. His classes were boring. Totally boring. There was almost no class discussion, no critical thinking. I decided to be a renegade. At home, I found my father's college textbook on American history, which was considerably more detailed and sophisticated than our high school text. I decided to read about various events in the college textbook before Mr. Erickson discussed them in class and to memorize critical dates and outcomes. Then, when Mr. Erickson lectured about the events in class, I was ready and eager to correct him if he made a mistake—or to provide additional detail if he did not do an event sufficient justice: "Mr. Erickson, I believe that the defender of the Boston Tea Party was Samuel Adams, not John Adams, as you stated. Samuel Adams and John Adams were second cousins." A few days later in class: "Mr. Erickson, I believe that the Battle of Saratoga took place during the fall of 1777, not during the spring as you mentioned. It had to be the fall because General Burgoyne did not start marching south from Quebec until June 13 and did not defeat the Americans at Fort Ticonderoga until July 7—and then he continued south to Saratoga, arriving in that area in mid-September." Finally, Mr. Erickson had had enough of me. He offered me a deal I could not refuse. Mr. Erickson was a neighbor and acquaintance of Henry A. Wallace, the former U.S. secretary of agriculture and vice president under Franklin Roosevelt. When serving as secretary of agriculture, Henry Wallace championed a plan he called the Ever-Normal Granary. Mr. Erickson's deal was that if I interviewed Henry Wallace and wrote a paper on the Ever-Normal

Granary, I would be excused from attending classes for the remainder of the semester. I accepted the deal in two seconds (it took me that long to say "yes"). Interviewing a former vice president of the United States was a heady proposition for a high school senior. Much better than attending a totally boring class.

The Ever-Normal Granary was a simple concept. When large crop sizes of corn, wheat, or soybeans led to surplus supplies and consequent down-ward pressures on prices, the government would intervene and purchase sufficient quantities of the crop to stabilize prices. The government would store the purchased inventories in granaries. Then, when small crop sizes led to threatened shortages and upward pressures on prices, the govern-ment would attempt to stabilize the market by selling part or all of the crop being held in the granaries. The government's actions to stabilize the agricultural markets theoretically would be good for both the farmer and the consumer. It was a win-win situation.

I had two interviews with Henry Wallace. Both went well, and I started to write the requisite paper. Mr. Erickson believed that the Ever-Normal Granary was an excellent concept and, of course, Henry Wallace was in love with it. I thought about the practicality of the Ever-Normal Granary and, with a sly sense of pleasure, arrived at a differing conclusion. My conclusion was that, if the government stabilized prices at a relatively high level in a year that farmers produced excess supplies of a crop, the farmers would have economic incentives to continue planting large quantities of the crop. Thus, except in rare times of poor weather, farmers would continually produce excess supplies that the government would have to purchase. Eventually, the granaries would be filled to capacity. And then what? Furthermore, if the government stabilized U.S. prices at artificially high levels, what would prevent importers from flooding the market with crops purchased at lower prices from other countries that also were experiencing surplus crops? The concept of the Ever-Normal Granary sounded good on paper, but I concluded that it simply would not work in practice. Mr. Erickson, of course, was not happy with my conclusion, and he made me promise that I would not share it with

Henry A. Wallace. So I was a 17-year-old contrarian to a former vice president of the United States—and to my teacher to boot. But I did receive an A+ as my final grade in American history, and I scored 97 on the final exam, even though I was absent from class for a large percentage of the semester.

I strongly believe that my willingness and ability to be a contrarian is part of my DNA.

2. MOTIVATION TO SUCCEED FINANCIALLY

At one time, there was considerable wealth in both my parents' families. But unfortunately or fortunately for my brother and me, most of the wealth was lost over the years.

My father's great-grandfather, Michael Sampter, became prosperous as the founder of M. Sampter & Sons, one of the first "ready-made" clothing companies. My grandmother, Elvie Grace Sampter Wachenheim, grew up in a Manhattan mansion with governesses and tutors. She vacationed with her parents and sister in Europe and spent summers at a family-owned lakefront estate in the Adirondacks, where an Indian guide from the Abenaki tribe led the Sampter girls on fishing, canoeing, and mountain climbing trips. However, by the time my grandmother was in her mid-teens, M. Sampter & Sons no longer was profitable[1] and much of the family fortune was lost.

In 1906, Elvie Sampter married Edgar Wachenheim, who at the time was a successful investment banker at Speyer & Co. Thus, my father, Edgar Jr., also grew up in a household of some wealth. However, the Great Depression changed the fortunes of the Wachenheim family. My grandfather shared in the profits and losses of Speyer & Co. By the mid-1930s, the profits had become losses, and my grandfather decided to stem his losses by retiring. While the senior Wachenheims remained wealthy by the standards of the 1930s, because of Speyer's losses in the early 1930s and because my grandfather retired at a relatively early age, he never became wealthy by today's standards.

On my mother's side of the family, my great-grandfather, Samuel "Boss" Davis, founded a cigar company that, by the early 1900s, had become, according to one of Boss's obituaries, "one of the best known and most prosperous cigar manufacturing establishments in the country." When Boss developed diabetes, he sold Samuel I. Davis & Co. to the American Tobacco Company for $1 million, then a large sum. Upon Boss's death in 1918 (diabetes usually was fatal before insulin was purified in the early 1920s), my great grandmother, Elizabeth "Biggie" Abohbot Davis, inherited the $1 million plus substantial other assets. Biggie largely invested her fortune in mortgages and fixed-income bonds and, for the next 36 years, spent a meaningful percentage of her fortune on luxuries, including the upkeep of a large apartment that overlooked New York City's Central Park. When I was a small child, I visited the apartment frequently. To this day, I have memories of dozens of large potted plants filling the spacious foyer and spilling over into adjoining rooms. To enter the large living room, one walked through a forest. A servant spent a large percentage of each day caring for the plants. Biggie's lavish lifestyle was unfortunate (pardon the pun) for the wealth of future generations. Upon Biggie's death in 1954, inheritance taxes were paid on what remained of her assets and the then residual was divided between her three daughters, with one-third going to my grandmother, Leonora "Lennie" Davis Lewis. Sadly, Lennie's husband contracted multiple sclerosis at a young age and could not work. Lennie had a sufficient income to live comfortably and to send my mother to private schools, but the Davis fortune largely was lost to poor fixed-income investment strategies, lavish spending, high taxes, and disease.

When I was growing up in the 1940s and 1950s, my parents' income consisted of my father's modest salary and some dividend and interest income from family trusts. My parents could afford to live in a nice neighborhood in New Rochelle, New York, and could afford some luxuries, but I was aware that they lived on a tight budget. They definitely were not close to being wealthy. I also was aware that there had been considerable wealth in the family and that the wealth had been lost. I am convinced that this knowledge motivated me to work hard in life to achieve financial success.

Would have I worked as hard if I had grown up in a mansion serviced by servants? Probably not, and my observations of families that are wealthy support this conclusion.

I strongly wish to add a paragraph in this book about values. My parents and grandparents were adherents of the ethics and values taught by the Ethical Culture Society, which is a quasi-religion that teaches morality and ethics. My mother attended the Ethical Culture–Fieldston school system from kindergarten through 12th grade. Certain values were ingrained in the character and conduct of my parents and grandparents—and, in turn, in my brother and me. We were taught that money should be used as an opportunity for achievement, not for vainglory. We were taught that one should care greatly about the welfare of other people and that one should not spend lavishly on oneself. With these values in mind, the present conspicuous consumption of many ultra-successful newly rich investment professionals makes me sick. Enough said.

3. EDUCATION

I was lucky enough to be continually stretched intellectually at rigorous schools and at demanding corporations. After two undergraduate years at MIT, I transferred to Williams College after deciding not to pursue a career in science. After Williams, at the suggestion of Harvard Business School, I accepted a job at IBM, where I was forced to quickly learn a sufficient amount about accounting and business to participate in selling and installing large computer systems. I then attended Harvard Business School, where I was exposed to three business cases per day, six days per week, for two school years. Upon graduating from Harvard, I worked (too) long hours as a securities analyst at Goldman Sachs. After three years at Goldman, I accepted a job at Central National–Gottesman Corporation (CN-G), which is owned by my wife's family. CN-G is a worldwide marketer and distributor of almost every grade of paper and pulp. In the 1920s, CN-G started investing some of its excess cash flows in the stock market—and by the 1950s the company had formed an Investment Management

Division headed by Arthur Ross. Mr. Ross, as he liked to be called because he was a most formal man of the very old school, was a particularly successful investor and a particularly demanding boss. Soon after I joined CN-G, Mr. Ross called me into his office: "Ed, you are not going to learn much sitting at your desk. You need to be on the boards of companies. You need to be on the boards of companies" (whenever Mr. Ross wished to emphasize a point, he repeated it at least twice, and sometimes thrice). Well, I was about 30 years old, had a crew cut, and looked about 21. No company of any size and quality would want a relatively inexperienced 30-year-old on its board. Groucho Marx once said, "I don't want to belong to any club that would accept me as a member," and I should have adopted the position that I would not want to be a member of any corporate board that would accept me as a director.

After much cajoling, three companies invited me to join their boards. Each was small. Each was weak. Each had serious problems. One was a small, publicly owned grocery chain located in Portland, Oregon. At the start of my first board meeting, I was given a warm welcome by the chairman and other directors. Then, as the meeting progressed, I quickly reached the conclusion that the company's earnings outlook was terrible, that the company's internal accounting controls were almost completely nonexistent, that the board therefore needed to meet monthly rather than quarterly, that I did not have the time to fly to Oregon for monthly meetings, and consequently that I should resign from the board posthaste— which I did. Alas, I was a director of the company for a grand total of one hour and forty-eight minutes. Maybe Groucho Marx was right.

I then went on the board of a lead smelting company but resigned after a few years because my Ethical Culture background was at odds with management's continual delays installing proper equipment to eliminate the emissions of poisonous lead dust from the smelters.

Finally, I went on the board of American Saint-Gobain, a manufacturer of glass that just had completed the construction of a brand new plate glass plant that immediately was obsoleted by the new and materially more efficient Pilkington float method of producing glass. American

Saint-Gobain's new plate glass plant was a spanking new watermill at a time when American manufacturers were beginning to tear down watermills in favor of steam engines. American Saint-Gobain then had to struggle to convert its new plant to Pilkington's technology without going broke first.

Thus, my experiences as a 30-year-old director of three marginal companies were trials by fire. However, Mr. Ross was correct. Being a director of marginal or submarginal publicly owned companies was a valuable educational experience that did make me a better investor. So thank you, Mr. Ross.

When Arthur Ross retired in 1979, I assumed responsibility for the Investment Management Division of CN-G and became a director of the parent company, which was run by my brother-in-law. Eight years later, my brother-in-law and I decided that paper and investments were two disparate businesses that best should be separated from each other. I then became the owner of the investment operations, which I renamed Greenhaven Associates. For the next three years, I solely managed money for the Gottesman and Wachenheim families, but eventually decided to manage money for some non–family members and for some not-for-profits as well.

4. ANALYTICAL SKILLS

All my life, I struggled with verbal skills, but had the innate ability to cut through complex math, science, and logic problems. I believe that this skill is part of my DNA and has been reinforced by my continuing rigorous education.

There is one part of my science background that I am not proud of, however. When in high school, I was asked to compete in the Westinghouse Science Talent Search. Competitors had to sit for an exam and then submit an original research project. As a 17-year old member of the New Rochelle High School varsity hockey team, my immature and unrealistic ambition was to become an NHL hockey star, not a scientist. Almost every afternoon, when the ponds were sufficiently frozen, I would drive to a nearby pond for a game of shinny hockey, often cutting a class or two or three or four in the process. I was a hockey player, not a budding scientist. I had neither the time nor the interest to spend afternoons in an indoor lab performing experiments for some dumb and stupid research project. Westinghouse definitely was a near-bottom priority. But I found a solution to having my cake and eating it too. I adopted the convenient thesis that inhalation of ozone would improve an athlete's performance. My brother and I had an old transformer from our Lionel electric toy train set. By crossing a wire attached to one of the transformer's two terminals to a wire attached to the other terminal, I could create sparks. I had read that sparks convert some of the oxygen in the air into ozone. I borrowed 10 test tubes and 10 corks from my school's chemistry lab. One day, I rushed home from school and crossed the transformer wires inside each of the test tubes, quickly corking each after removing the wires. I then grabbed my skates and a stopwatch. Reaching Larchmont Reservoir, I laced my skates and then placed two sticks on the ice about 200 yards apart. I gave the stopwatch to a friend and instructed him (my trusty research assistant) to start the watch when I said "go" and stop the watch when I said "stop." I then uncorked two of the test tubes, placing the open end of each to each of my nostrils. Luckily, nobody, except my friend, saw me do this. Otherwise, they would have sent me to a lunatic asylum or worse. I inhaled the ozone from the two test tubes, skated to the starting stick, said "go," raced as fast as I could to the finishing stick, and, upon reaching it, said "stop." I repeated this procedure four more times. Then, without the benefit of either the ozone or much rest, I raced five more times between the two sticks. That was my control data. Voila, I had skated faster after inhaling the ozone than during the subsequent five control skates. I had proved beyond my doubt (but nobody else's) that ozone is a performance enhancer. Thoughts of glamour ran though my head. Maybe I would win first place in the Westinghouse. Maybe I would be the youngest person ever to win the Nobel Prize in Chemistry. I could see the headlines in the *New York Times:* "Seventeen-year-old Edgar Wachenheim III, star rookie center for the New York Rangers, was unanimously awarded the 1955

Nobel Prize in Chemistry for his pioneering work on the use of ozone to enhance athletic performance."

Of course, in reality, my research project probably was the worst ever performed in the entire long history of the Westinghouse Science Talent Search, and my chemistry teacher summarily rejected it long before it was to be submitted to Westinghouse. "Wachenheim," the teacher criticized, "did it ever occur to you that exhaustion might have played a role in your slower times during the last five skates? Wachenheim," the teacher continued, "did it ever occur to you that the small amount of electricity released by the transformer is totally insufficient to convert any oxygen into ozone? Thunderstorms, yes. Toy Lionel transformers, no. Wachenheim, I hope you play hockey better than you perform scientific experiments." And to complete the return to reality, not only did I fail to earn any prize in the Westinghouse, but I was not even elected to the 1955 Westchester County High School All-Star Hockey Team. So much for the Nobel Prize. So much for playing in the NHL. Dreams lost to reality. But it is far better for adolescents to dwell on dreams of future glory than to go through youth without ambitions—without passions.

5. CONFIDENCE

Because I was a strong student of math and science (in spite of the Westinghouse folly) who continually tested high for both achievement and aptitude, I gradually developed confidence in my innate analytical skills. This confidence was reinforced at Harvard Business School when, after my first year of study, I was elected a Baker Scholar. First-year Baker Scholars are those students whose grade average is among the top 2 percent in their class.

By the time I became responsible for managing portfolios of stocks, I was confident that I had the skill sets to become a successful investor. Importantly, this confidence gives me the ability to be a contrarian and to make decisions that are counter to the prevailing wisdom.

I am aware, however, that investment success can breed overconfidence and a resulting unrealistically low assessment of risk. Luckily, I have made a sufficient number of mistakes in my life that there is little danger that I will become overconfident. In my opinion, a good investor needs to strike the right balance between confidence and humility.

6. PRAGMATIC GOALS AND AMBITION

Lucius Annaeus Seneca, the Roman philosopher and statesman, once said: "If one does not know to which port one is sailing, no wind is favorable." I agree that investors should develop sensible and realistic goals. My goals have been to achieve average annual returns of 15 to 20 percent over the longer term without taking large risks of permanent loss.

I wish to emphasize the words *longer term*. Most hedge funds, mutual funds, and other investors are under pressure to please their clients by achieving favorable results in the short term. Many of these investors will shun (or even sell) a stock that has an uncertain short-term potential, even if the shares appear to be an excellent investment for the longer term. We are disinterested in short-term results and thus have the luxury of focusing our research and purchases on the much less competitive universe of stocks that have less promise of near-term appreciation, but that have exciting longer-term potential. This gives us a competitive edge.

I note that achieving relatively low volatility is not a goal. However, because I tend to purchase undervalued securities of high-quality companies with strong balance sheets, over the years our portfolios have experienced less volatility than the stock market has. The lower volatility has been the outcome, not the objective.

7. CONTROL OF EMOTIONS

Over the years, I have learned to control my emotions, especially when the prices of some or all of our stocks are falling sharply. I believe that part of the control is due to experience (I have been through so many bear markets that I am used to them) and part to my DNA. I simply find that, during times of stress, I am able to keep a relatively level head and to continue to think and act rationally.

8. FUN

I enjoy researching companies, I enjoy the thrills of generating creative ideas, and I enjoy making money. It is fun to come to the office most mornings. I am convinced that all this makes me a better investor.

• • •

The following timeline of my life might be helpful in understanding my investment career:

1937: Born in New York City.

1955: Graduated from high school and enrolled at MIT.

1957: Transferred to Williams College.

1959: Graduated from Williams College and went to work for IBM.

1962: Married Sue Ann Wallach; the first of our four children was born a year later.

1964: Enrolled at Harvard Business School.

1966: Graduated from Harvard and started working for Goldman Sachs.

1969: Accepted a job offer at Central National–Gottesman, Inc. (CN-G), a paper and investment management company owned by my wife's family (my wife's mother was a Gottesman).

1979: Became chief investment officer at CN-G.

1987: Spun off the investment management operations of CN-G into a new company, Greenhaven Associates, which I own. Greenhaven manages portfolios of common stocks for my family, my wife's family, and a limited number of non–family members.

NOTES

1. The history of M. Sampter & Sons is instructive. Until the invention of the sewing machine in 1853, a family's clothing usually was made by hand by the housewife or by a local seamstress to the individual specifications of the person who would be wearing the clothing. The invention of the sewing machine sharply reduced the costs

of making clothing. After the invention, it became more economical to mass produce large quantities of clothes to meet anticipated orders rather than to produce a single item to fulfill an order in hand, even if some of the mass-produced items later had to be marked down or discarded due to lack of demand for their size or style. In 1860, Michael Sampter formed his "ready-made" clothing company to take advantage of the changed economics. M. Sampter & Sons prospered for the first several decades after its founding. Pioneers tend initially to develop experiences and reputations that yield advantages over new competition. However, by the turn of the twentieth century, the manufacturing of clothes had become commodity-like, very competitive, and much less profitable—and M. Sampter & Sons floundered. The commoditization of products and manufacturing processes is normal. It is said that all products eventually become toasters.

3

IBM

In 1914, Thomas Watson, a star salesman for the National Cash Resister Company, was hired by the Computing-Tabulating-Recording Company (CTR) to be its president. CTR had been founded three years earlier to produce electromechanical machines that could "read" the location of holes in punched cards and make calculations and tabulations based on the location of the holes. For the first time, machines were replacing pencils for accounting applications. Watson was a super salesman and leader, and soon CTR became the world leader in tabulating office machines. In 1924, Watson, with infinite wisdom, changed the name of Computing-Tabulating-Recording to International Business Machines.

IBM's punched card equipment was a great success, and by the 1940s IBM was the world's dominant producer of office business machines. The business leased the punched card equipment under full-service leases that included maintenance and technical advice as well as the equipment itself. IBM's strong financial incentive was to keep each piece of equipment on lease for as long as possible. While IBM earned good profits during the early years of a lease, if the equipment remained on lease after it was fully depreciated, IBM's profits became particularly large. Thus, IBM had incentives to delay the introduction of new, more efficient equipment that would obsolete and replace existing equipment on lease.

Over the decades, a number of inventors produced electromechanical machines that were at least somewhat programmable. These were called computers. IBM's first computer was delivered to Harvard University on August 7, 1944, for use by the U.S. Navy Bureau of Ships. IBM called the computer the Automatic Sequence Controlled Calculator. But Harvard simply and wisely called it the Mark 1. For the next seven years, IBM had little incentive to introduce programmable machines for the commercial market. After all, it did not wish to obsolete its highly profitable line of punched card equipment. However, in 1951, the Remington Rand Corporation delivered its first UNIVAC computer—and IBM saw the handwriting on the wall. IBM knew that if it did not introduce its own line of commercial computers, its punched card equipment eventually would be replaced by UNIVACs, or by computers made by other companies.

In 1952, IBM introduced its 701 vacuum tube computer, and the race was on. But it never was a close race. It was a cheetah against a sloth. IBM benefited from vastly superior research, engineering, marketing, and applications knowhow. Furthermore, computer users felt safe with IBM. Computers were new and complex, and corporations installing computers relied on the computer manufacturer for technical and applications expertise. IBM was a highly respected and known quantity. If a corporate executive selected an IBM system and the installation developed problems, the corporate executive could blame IBM for the problems. However, if a corporate executive selected a non-IBM computer and the installation developed problems, the corporate executive could be blamed by his bosses for selecting a second- or third-tier computer company, and the executive's career could be in jeopardy. Thus, the vast majority of executives played it safe and stuck with IBM. UNIVAC, GE, RCA, Honeywell, and Burroughs often could offer more cost-efficient computers, but IBM usually received the orders. This was particularly true after IBM introduced its technologically advanced System/360 family of compatible computers in

1964. The 360s were efficient, reliable, user friendly—and carried the IBM brand. IBM had a winner.

The System/360 transformed IBM into one of the most successful corporations ever. Between 1964 and 1974, the company's revenues grew at a 14.6 percent average annual rate from $3.23 billion to $12.67 billion. Net earnings grew even faster, at a 17.5 percent rate, from $364 million to $1,830 million. IBM's market share during the period approached 80 percent. Competitors could not compete, and some quit. GE sold its computer business to Honeywell in 1970. One year later, RCA sold its computer business to Sperry Rand.

The seeds for IBM's eventual downfall came in 1972, when Intel developed its first microprocessor, the 4004. A microprocessor incorporates the functions of a computer's complex inner workings on a single integrated circuit, or, at most, on a few integrated circuits. The first microprocessors were not sufficiently powerful to challenge the viability of IBM's System/360s and other mainframe computers. However, Intel cofounder Gordon Moore famously had predicted: "The number of transistors incorporated in a chip will approximately double every 24 months"—and Gordon Moore proved correct. By the late 1970s, microprocessors were sufficiently powerful that relatively inexpensive desktop computers could start replacing expensive mainframes. In 1977, Apple introduced the first successful desktop (personal) computer, the Apple II. The Apple II was a hit. Eventually, 1.25 million were sold. IBM noticed this success and noticed that microprocessor technology was progressing so rapidly that IBM's mainframe business, which was the source of most of the company's profits, was in jeopardy of being obsoleted. IBM had to respond.

In 1981, IBM introduced the IBM Personal Computer to replace its unpopular 5200 desktop computer. The IBM PC, backed by IBM's reputation for excellence, was a hit and helped drive IBM's sales and profits in the early 1980s.

Other events also drove IBM's reported profits in the early 1980s. In 1980, John Opel became CEO of the company (Tom Watson had retired in 1956 and Tom Watson Jr. had retired in 1971 after suffering a heart attack). Opel was concerned about IBM's policy that a leased computer could be returned to IBM by a customer with 30 days' notice. His prime worry was that competitors, using advanced microprocessor technology, would start marketing computers that were materially more cost effective than IBM's mainframes. IBM's mainframe customers would then cancel their leases with IBM, leaving IBM with substantially reduced profits and with inventories of relatively new, but technologically obsolete, computers. Responding to these concerns, Opel changed IBM's pricing policy by offering to sell used mainframes at deeply discounted prices. The low prices encouraged customers to purchase the mainframes they were leasing. By doing this, IBM immediately received revenues (the sales price of the used computer) and profits that would have been received in later years if the computer had remained on lease. Thus, as long as customers converted leases into sales, IBM's reported revenues and profits were artificially inflated. Then, when the rate of conversions slowed, IBM changed its terms on new leases that permitted the company to treat the leases as full payout leases. On full payout leases, most of the expected revenues and profits could be booked when the computers were delivered to the customers. Previously, the revenues and profits were booked over the life of the leases.

The introduction of personal computers, the conversion of leases to sales, and the new accounting for leases caused IBM's revenues and earnings to surge between 1980 and 1985. During the five-year period, revenues increased at a 13.8 percent average annual rate from $26.21 billion to $50.05 billion and net profits increased at a 14.1 percent average rate from $3.39 billion to $6.55 billion. IBM shareholders had much to be thankful for. The price of IBM's shares, adjusted for subsequent stock splits, rose from $16.09 at year-end 1979 to $38.88 at year-end 1985.

However, all really was not well. Not well at all. When IBM developed its lines of personal computers, it adopted Intel's chip technology and Microsoft's MS-DOS operating system. This was a convenience. However, because other personal computer manufacturers had equal access to Intel's chips and Microsoft's operating system, IBM lost any hope of significant product differentiation, and personal computers rapidly became commodities that were sold based on price. Over time, Dell, Compaq, and other PC manufacturers with lower cost structures than IBM would be able to outcompete IBM.

IBM was facing additional problems as well. Computer power was increasing rapidly and was becoming less expensive. Moore's law was working. By the mid-1980s, personal computers could perform many of the jobs previously performed by mainframes. Furthermore, Digital Equipment's line of VAX minicomputers also was taking market share from IBM's mainframes. In addition, while in the 1960s companies heavily relied on IBM's technical expertise and reputation, by the mid-1980s many corporations had sufficient in-house expertise and experience that they no longer needed to rely on IBM. In the 1960s, IBM had pricing power, but by the mid-1980s the company often had to price competitively to win orders.

When relatively nondifferentiable products are sold based on their price, the manufacturers of the products normally need to have low cost structures if they wish to be competitive and earn reasonable profits. Unfortunately, largely because of its history, IBM's cost structure was high—very high. In the 1960s, IBM needed large numbers of salesmen and technical advisers to sell and install mainframes. It also needed large numbers of maintenance engineers to provide maintenance and repairs to its mainframes, which were not nearly as reliable as computers produced 20 years later. By the mid-1980s, a large percentage of IBM's sales managers, salesmen, applications programmers, technical advisers, and maintenance engineers were superfluous, but IBM maintained a policy of not laying off any employee as long as he was not incompetent or dishonest. Many superfluous employees were "promoted" upstairs to corporate headquarters to perform such less essential or nonessential tasks as competitive analysis, sales forecasting, quality control, real estate management, corporate relations, investor relations, community relations, and economic forecasting. In short, IBM's cost structure was bloated at a time when the company's revenues and gross margins were under pressure from systemic adverse technological changes in the computer business.

IBM's revenues continued to increase some in the late 1980s, but fell far short of the company's earlier hopes. In 1984, John Opel predicted that the company's revenues would reach $100 billion in 1990. Actual 1990 revenues were $69 billion. Earnings fared far worse than revenues. After-tax earnings in 1990 were $6.02 billion, 8 percent below the level of five years earlier. And the price of IBM's shares even fared far worse than earnings, declining 27 percent between the last trading day of 1985 and the last trading day of 1990.

John Akers replaced John Opel as CEO on February 1, 1985, at a time when IBM was bloated with more than 400,000 employees. In 1985, I was invited by Jon Rotenstreich, IBM's treasurer, to have lunch at the company's headquarters in Armonk, New York. Jon is a friend who previously had been a managing director of Salomon Brothers. We had lunch in the company's central dining room. Jon looked around the dining room and pointed out employee after employee who came to the office every morning, but essentially had little work to do. "See that guy over there with the green tie? He used to be a regional sales manager. Now he is a community relations specialist. He comes to the office at about 10 and grabs a cup of coffee. He is responsible for IBM's relations with the hamlet of Armonk, so it is important for him to read the local Armonk weekly newspaper and watch for local Armonk news on TV. That takes him the rest of the day, except for a two-hour lunch break and three or four additional coffee breaks. Get the picture?" I got the picture. Jon strongly hoped that John Akers would abandon IBM's policy of lifetime employment and would substantially reduce IBM's payroll and other costs.

Akers formed several task forces to study IBM and its future. The task forces' findings were worrisome. They concluded that IBM was in a state of decline. After reviewing the findings, Akers initiated a series of early retirement programs, offering large severance packages to employees willing to leave the company. Of course, many of the most capable employees—those readily able to find other jobs quickly—accepted the package. So IBM lost a lot of talent and kept a lot of deadwood (adverse selection at work). Furthermore, in spite of the retirement programs, IBM's employment levels only declined from 405,000 at the end of 1985 to 374,000 at the end of 1990. During that period, IBM's fundamentals deteriorated faster than its employment levels. By 1990, for about $100,000 a computer user could purchase a workstation that had the power of a mainframe that several years earlier had sold for a few million dollars. IBM suffered a large operating loss in 1991. Akers then had to act, and he did so by increasing the size of the retirement programs. IBM's employment levels declined to 344,000 at the end of 1991 and to 302,000 at the end of 1992. However, IBM still had far too many employees, morale was poor, and the company continued to lose money.

I became interested in seriously thinking about IBM's shares in 1985 after my lunch with Jon Rotenstreich. My initial analysis was straightforward. IBM no longer was a growth company with competitive advantages that led to high profit margins. Thus, it no longer deserved to sell at a high price-to-earnings (PE) ratio. However, if the company could become cost competitive by sharply reducing its head count and by selling excess plants and office buildings, it could emerge as a large and powerful company that should earn a reasonable return on revenues. Furthermore, the company would not have to spend large sums to build new plants—and, therefore, a large percentage of its future earnings would be available for dividends or share repurchases.

When I become interested in studying a company, I sometimes quickly purchase a few shares of the company's stock. Ownership incentivizes me to study the company with increased intensity. I purchased a few shares of IBM on two occasions between 1989 and 1992, but sold the shares each time because I believed that IBM's problems could deteriorate further before they started to improve. The second time I sold the shares following a meeting with John Akers in his office. The legendary investor Mike Steinhardt owned shares of IBM. Mike knew that I also owned shares, and he invited me to join him in a meeting he had scheduled with Akers. It took me one second to say "yes" to the invitation. However, the meeting turned out to be discombobulated because Mike and I had completely different reasons for being interested in IBM. Mike observed that the company had a very profitable and rapidly growing subsidiary in Japan. In 1991, Japanese companies still sold at high PE ratios. Mike wanted IBM to spin off its Japanese subsidiary to IBM shareholders. He reasoned that the Japanese subsidiary alone would be worth a large percentage of IBM's existing market value and that the combined market value of the two pieces (IBM Japan and IBM ex-Japan) would be far in excess of IBM's existing share price. I doubted the practicability of dividing IBM into two separate companies. Instead, I questioned Akers on why IBM was not reducing costs more aggressively. One minute Mike was asking about Japan, and the next minute I was asking about costs. Then, Mike had another thought about spinning out Japan, and then I had a thought about weeding out the dead-wood as opposed to incentivizing the most capable to leave IBM. It went back and forth for a full hour. Akers could not have been more courteous, but it was clear to me that he was not going to cut costs more aggressively— and it was very clear to me that he was not going to spin out Japan.

IBM was doing poorly. Akers was under pressure and, in early 1993, announced his resignation. Lou Gerstner was his replacement. IBM held a press conference on the day Gerstner assumed control. Gerstner, who was wearing a very unlike-IBM blue shirt, told the audience of reporters that he had the courage to take tough steps. That is what I wanted to hear. I decided to seriously consider making a large investment in IBM's shares.

My analysis was roughly as follows. I estimated that that company had about 60,000 more employees than needed and that an average employee's compensation (salary and benefits) totaled about $85,000. Therefore, I concluded that Gerstner might be able to reduce costs by $5 billion. After taxes at a 32 percent effective rate, the cost reductions would add about $3.4 billion to net earnings, or about $1.50 per share based on the 2.29 billion IBM shares that were outstanding. Before nonrecurring charges, IBM was roughly breaking even at the time. Therefore, I estimated that the company's current earnings power would be about $1.50 per share pro forma a $5 billion reduction in costs. I further estimated that the company's revenues would grow at a 5 percent rate and therefore that IBM's earnings power in 1995 could be about $1.65 per share. When we purchase a stock, we are interested in what the company will be worth two or three years hence, so the $1.65 was an important number.

In order to check the reasonableness of earnings estimates, I often like to use two disparate methodologies when projecting earnings – and then see if the two methodologies reach similar conclusions. In the case of IBM, I decided to also use the following thought process. The company's revenues in 1993 were expected to be about $63 billion. Assuming a 5 percent growth rate, revenues in 1995 would be about $69 million. Based on my experience, I estimated that an efficient manufacturer of computers that was operating in a competitive environment might have after-tax profit margins of 5 to 6 percent. Based on this methodology, IBM's after-tax earnings power in 1995 would be $3.5 to $4.1 billion, or $1.50 to $1.80 per share.

I decided to use $1.65 as a single best estimate of what IBM's earnings power could be in 1995. Finally, to value the shares, I assigned a multiple to the $1.65. I believed that IBM's quality and growth potential were somewhat below average. Since I believe that an average company is worth 15 to 16 times earnings, I valued IBM at 12 to 13 times earnings. Thus, I estimated that, in 1995, the shares would be worth $20 to $21. I knew that my projections of IBM's earnings and values were nothing more than best guesses based on incomplete information. However, having the projections to work with was better than not having any projections at all, and my experience is that a surprisingly large percentage of our earnings and valuation projections eventually are achieved, although often we are far off on the timing.

IBM's shares were selling at $12 at the time I completed my analysis in May 1993. Over the next two months, I purchased a substantial position in the shares at an average cost of about $11½. We usually purchase stocks because we believe that one or more positive changes will trigger a sharp appreciation in the price of the stocks. In this case, we hoped that IBM would announce a definitive plan to substantially reduce its costs.

On July 28, Lou Gerstner announced a plan to reduce employment levels to 225,000 by the end of the year. About 85,000 employees, or slightly more than 25 percent of the existing workforce, would leave by year-end. Several months after the announcement, both Lou Gerstner and his cost-reduction program started to gain credibility on Wall Street. In November, IBM's shares started to appreciate. By August 1994, the shares were selling at about $15½. By that time, the common wisdom on Wall Street was that Gerstner's cost-reduction program had been successful. It appeared that the company would earn about $1.25 per share in 1994 and materially more in 1995.

My strategy is to purchase shares in anticipation of a positive change and then, normally, to sell the shares when the change occurs and is largely discounted into the price of the shares. In the case of IBM, the change had occurred and investor sentiment had turned largely positive. At the time we had purchased the shares at about $11½ the sentiment had been decidedly negative. Because of the change in sentiment, I decided to sell our position, which we accomplished over the next few months at an average price of just above $16. We earned a 40 percent profit in the stock. Yes, I had estimated that the shares might be worth $20 to $21 in 1995, but a bird in the hand is worth two in the bush—and I was happy to realize the 40 percent profit.

Selling the shares turned out to be a big mistake because my analysis had been incomplete. In 1994 and in following years, IBM generated large amounts of excess cash. While a small portion of the cash was used for acquisitions, the largest portion was used to repurchase shares. IBM's average diluted share count declined by 1.7 percent in 1995, and then by 8.5 percent in 1996, and by another 7.4 percent in 1997. As a result, IBM's per-share earnings increased materially faster than its net earnings. I had failed to consider the repurchases. Also, my estimate that the company's after-tax profit margins should be 5 to 6 percent proved to be too conservative. In 1996, the company's after-tax margin was 7 percent, and IBM was on track to earn about 2.50 per share in that year.

In very late 1995 and in early 1996, I swallowed hard and rebuilt a large position in IBM's shares at an average cost of about $24½. My reasoning was that the combination of the share repurchases and the improved margins would lead to higher earnings per share (EPS) than was generally predicted by Wall Street.

While I was very wrong to sell the shares in 1994 at about $16, I was very right to purchase them again 15 months later. IBM earned $2.51 per share in 1996 and $3.01 per share in 1997, and the price of the shares increased sharply in response to the improved earnings. I sold the shares in late 1997 at an average price of about $48. Again, my timing was far less than perfect. In mid-1999, the shares traded above $60.

Over the years, I have learned that we can do well in the stock market if we do enough things right and if we avoid large permanent losses, but that it is impossible to do nearly everything right. To err is human—and I make plenty of errors. My judgment to sell IBM's shares in 1993 at $16 was an expensive mistake. I try not to fret over mistakes. If I did fret, the investment process would be less enjoyable and more stressful. In my opinion, investors do best when they are relaxed and are having fun.

I continued to follow IBM after we sold the shares. The company struggled to grow. During the 15-year period from 1998 to 2013, IBM's revenues grew at only a 1.3 percent compound annual growth rate (CAGR), from $81.7 billion to $99.8 billion. IBM, once one of the most respected growth companies in the world, now was a mature, slow growth company selling commodity-like products and services.

Warren Buffett wrote in Berkshire Hathaway's 1998 annual report that, when Berkshire owns shares of a wonderful business, "our favorite holding period is forever." I greatly admire Warren Buffett. He is one of the great investors of all time. But I strongly disagree that the shares of most wonderful businesses can be held forever because most wonderful businesses become less wonderful over time—and many eventually run into difficulties. IBM is one example of why most stocks cannot be held forever. Kodak is another example. Coca-Cola, which is one of Berkshire Hathaway's largest holdings, is a third example. Over the 10-year period 2003 to 2013, Coca-Cola's revenues and EPS increased at CAGRs of 8.3 percent and

7.1 percent, and the price of its shares increased at only a 4.9 percent CAGR. Coca-Cola once was a rapidly growing company. More recently, its markets seem to have matured. Greenhaven strives to achieve annual returns of 15 to 20 percent. It would be near impossible to earn returns anywhere near 15 percent by continually holding shares in a company that is growing 7 to 8 percent per year. My job would be a lot easier and much more relaxing if I could fill a portfolio with outstanding companies that I never would sell. But our ambitions lead us to seek shares that are temporarily deeply undervalued and then sell the shares when they become fully valued. This is an approach to investing that is less relaxing and that requires considerable effort and time, but that has worked for us.

Thus, being a successful value investor is time consuming. There always is another company to study, another periodical to read. I sometimes am asked how I allocate my time. What exactly does an investment manager do? Acknowledging that other managers likely spend their time very differently than I do, the following is an example of how I might spend a typical workday. The example is representative but not completely factual. I awaken at about 5:00 a.m. and, after shaving, exercising, showering, and dressing, walk down the hall to my home office, which is equipped with a Bloomberg. This particular morning, my first business of the day is to search the Bloomberg for general business and world news. I then review a model of FedEx's projected earnings that I was working on the previous evening. I am tired when I finish the model at about 9:30 p.m. and promise myself that I will take a fresh look at the model after a good night's sleep. After rethinking some of my assumptions and estimates, I make some inconsequential changes to the model and print out a copy. I then write a one-page memo that explains the model and summarizes my conclusions about the value of the shares. After proofreading the memo, I pack my briefcase, grab a bowl of cereal, and head to Greenhaven's offices in Purchase, New York, which are located about 15 minutes from our home in Rye.

Upon arriving at our Purchase offices at just after 7:00, I give a copy of the FedEx memo and model to my assistant to distribute to Greenhaven's three securities analysts (my son Chris, Josh Sandbulte, and me) and to the firm's trader. I wish to keep my associates fully informed about my thinking. I will keep my copy in a nearby file so that I can refer to it in the future whenever I am working on the company.

I then notice that our trader, Eli, has placed a number of press releases and brokerage reports on my desk. Eli usually arrives at the offices at about 6:30 and immediately searches the Bloomberg for any news or Wall Street reports that may be of interest to us. He distributes hard copies of the news and analysts' reports to Chris, Josh, and me. I scan the hard copies for any relevant new news or ideas. There is none. There rarely is. But I am interested in the opinions of the Wall Street analysts, not because they will directly influence an investment decision, but because they collectively reflect the conventional wisdom on a security and therefore help me understand why a security is selling at the price at which it is selling.

After scanning the press releases and analysts' reports, I use a function on the Bloomberg to receive the latest news on our holdings and prospective holdings. Then (usually about 7:30 to 7:45), I get together with Chris and Josh to discuss anything that any of us wishes to discuss, varying from what we are working on, to news or ideas, to suggested purchases or sales for the day, to brainstorming for ideas. Some days the meetings are only about 15 minutes long. On other days they can last for an hour or more. At this morning's meeting, we have a long discussion about FedEx. For several quarters the company's results lagged our expectations, but very recently the company's fundamentals have improved. Does the improvement indicate that our thesis on the company is beginning to work? At the end of the meeting, Chris reminds me that the newly appointed CFO of 3M, Nick Gangestad, is telephoning us at 11:00. I tell Chris that we should get together at 10:45 to organize the questions we will ask on the call.

It now is almost 8:30. I scan a computer printout that gives me the holdings of each of our 150 or so accounts by percentage. For example, Mary Jones's account breaks down as follows: 9.2 percent of the current value of her account is invested in FedEx, 8.2 percent in UPS, 9.0 percent in Lowe's, and so on. I have decided that each of Greenhaven's accounts should have at least a 9.5 percent holding in FedEx and I have noticed that some of our accounts own slightly less than 9.5 percent. I tell our trader Eli to bring each of our accounts' holdings in FedEx up to 9.5 percent, but only if the account has sufficient cash to do so. Eli can use his computer to determine how much FedEx he will be purchasing for each account. We try to be as automated as possible. The purchase of a relatively small number of FedEx shares will be my only order for the day. Because we tend to hold stocks for two to five years, our trading often is light—and on many days we do not buy or sell a single share of stock.

It is now 8:45. I am interested in adding to our holdings of stocks that will benefit from an expected upturn in the housing market. Previously and repeatedly, I have screened for housing-related companies that have market values in excess of $5 billion and that appear to be undervalued, but to no avail. Today, I will run a screen of housing-related companies that have market values of $3 to $5 billion. Because we have $5.4 billion under management, we normally need to focus on companies that have market values in excess of $5 billion, but I am frustrated to find an additional attractive housing-related stock, and I will try almost anything to find one. I use a function on the Bloomberg to identify companies that fulfill my industry and size criteria. After briefly considering dozens of names that appear on the screen, I write down the stock ticker symbols of five companies that might merit some analysis. Again using the Bloomberg, I pull down the Form 10-K[1] of one of the companies and then start analyzing its balance sheet and reading a description of its business activities. Time passes quickly. It is now 10:15. I cease reading about the housing-related company and pull out my file on 3M. Before speaking to the company's new CFO, I need to review my previous memos and notes on the company and carefully and thoughtfully prepare a list of questions that will be most helpful to our analysis—and that the CFO is likely to answer. After decades of speaking to managements, I have improved my skills on what questions to ask and how to ask them.

At 10:45, Chris enters my office. We spend about 10 minutes discussing the questions we will ask 3M's CFO. Then, as we wait for the phone to ring, I ask Eli how our FedEx order is progressing. He responds that we had only 54,000 shares to purchase and that the order was completed at 10:20—and that the shares are up $.10 from our average purchase price. Soon the phone rings. It is the CFO, Nick Gangestad, himself, not his assistant. I amusingly find that the highest-level executives in a company often place and receive calls themselves without the aid of assistants, while lower-level employees tend to use assistants in order to make themselves appear more important. After congratulating Nick on his promotion, I ask questions about his background, from the time he was a child until his promotion as CFO. He grew up on a 1,280-acre farm in Iowa and apparently had a wholesome upbringing, often working with his hands on farm chores. We then spend at least 45 minutes discussing 3M. I focus on areas that seem to be the most critical determinants of what the company will be worth in two or three years. I ask whether the slower economic growth in the developing parts of the world will cause the company to reduce its growth goals or whether the slower growth already was anticipated by the company when it established its goals. I then ask whether the highly profitable and rapidly growing health care segment can hold its operating margins above 30 percent. I also ask whether the company plans to increase its prices outside the United States if foreign currencies (and especially the euro and yen) decline in value versus the U.S. dollar. We then discuss the company's share repurchase program and its projected pension expense. Originally, the company had expected that its annual pension expense would decline to close to zero by 2017, but Chris learned that the actuarial tables used to compute pension expense are being altered to reflect the longer life expectancy of Americans, and this alteration will cause the future pension expense of many companies to be materially larger than previously expected.

After the call ends, Chris and I review what we learned, and decide we are hungry and it is time for lunch. Frequently, Chris, Josh, and I lunch at a nearby restaurant. Today, we lunch at a local country club, where the food is good and the service is quick. Chris and I fill Josh in on our call with Nick Gangestad, and then we spend the rest of lunchtime brainstorming about industries and companies that might indirectly be helped by an upturn in the housing market. We do not come up with any worthwhile ideas. We usually strike out when we brainstorm. But we only need a handful of good ideas a year—and we keep trying.

We return to the office at 1:45. Mary, my assistant, tells me that Todd Corbin, the chief investment officer of the New York Public Library, telephoned while I was out. I am chair of the library's Investment Committee, which is responsible for the its $1.1 billion endowment, and Todd is the library's full-time employee who suggests strategies, recommends outside investment managers, and continually monitors the outside managers. At the previous committee meeting, I had raised a theoretical question. What, if anything, should the library do if the stock market climbs to excessive heights? Should the library hedge the stock market or ask some of its managers to sell part or all of the equities they hold in the library's account? While I was not predicting that the stock market would climb to excessive levels, I thought it would be beneficial if we researched our options now so that we would be best prepared to act in the future should the market rise sharply from present levels. I gave Todd and each committee member a homework assignment to think about our options and strategies. Neil Rudenstine, the former president of Harvard University, is a member of the Investment Committee, as is Tony Marx, the former president of Amherst College. After giving out the homework assignment, I chuckled out loud and said: "You know, when I was a student at Williams College, I was in absolute awe of the college's president—he was a godlike figure—and it would have been beyond my wildest dreams that someday I would be handing out homework assignments to the former president of Harvard and to the former president of Amherst."

I talk to Todd for about one hour. Protecting the portfolio might be more difficult than hoped. A small percentage of our equities are held in discrete accounts, but the bulk is held in pooled accounts. We can ask the managers of the discrete accounts to raise cash, but we have no control over the pooled accounts—and we would not wish to withdraw our funds from the pooled accounts because the managers are good and most of them are no longer accepting new accounts. Therefore, if we withdraw the funds, we likely would not be able to reinvest with them once we decided to again increase our exposure to equities. Todd had checked on the practicability of purchasing put options on the S&P 500 Index, but the options seem to be prohibitively expensive. He also checked on shorting the Standard & Poor's (S&P) 500 Index, but to do so the library would have to provide cash as collateral for any unrealized losses. Few things in life are easy. Todd said he would keep looking for ideas.

I did not mind spending an hour with Todd. Over the years, I have spent considerable time with not-for-profits. Being on boards and committees is worthwhile, but chairing committees is particularly worthwhile because the buck stops with you and therefore you are forced to become actively engaged. Over the years, I have chaired five investment committees, one executive committee, two finance committees, one audit committee, one art curatorial committee (at the Museum of Modern Art), two capital campaigns, and two boards of trustees. In each case, I learned more than I gave—and what I learned has made me a better investor.

The call with Todd ends. It is about 2:45. I return to analyzing the five smaller housing-related companies. I reject the first because it seems to be a higher-cost producer of undifferentiated products. I reject the second and third because their balance sheets and cash flows do not seem sufficiently strong. The time is now 3:45. I usually leave the office at 3:45 to 4:00. I check my calendar for the following day, pack my briefcase with all my material on 3M, and leave for Rye.

Arriving home at 4:00, I read the mail, take a shower, and change into comfortable clothes. I then return to my home office. From 4:45 until dinnertime at 6:15, I think about 3M and our conversation with Nick Gangestad, and I start revising my principal memo on the company. After dinner, I complete the revision of the memo and then update my earnings model. I review our reasons for owning the shares and our valuation. I remain happy we own the shares. By now, it is close to 9:45. I am tired. It is time for bed.

NOTES

1. The Form 10-K is a document that every publicly traded company files annually with the Securities and Exchange Commission. The document contains detailed information about the company's business and financial statements.

4

INTERSTATE BAKERIES

In 1905, 18-year-old Ralph Leroy Nafziger started baking breads in the basement of a church in downtown Kansas City. The breads were good and sold well. The success motivated Nafziger to build and purchase a number of real bakeries. Twenty years later, he sold the bakeries to a competitor, but soon afterwards used the proceeds from the sale to purchase a number of other bakeries that, in 1930, he combined to form Interstate Bakeries. Over the next 30 years, Nafziger acquired 15 additional bakeries, building Interstate into one of the largest bread and snack cake companies in the United States.

Interstate's business included distribution and marketing as well as baking. Bread has a relatively short shelf life. Therefore, it must be delivered to stores soon after it is baked. To accomplish this, in the 1980s, Interstate operated a fleet of more than 3,000 delivery vehicles that transported its breads and other baked products to tens of thousands of supermarkets, smaller grocery stores, convenience stores, and restaurants. The drivers of the vehicles, who belonged to the Teamsters union, placed the newly baked products on the shelves and removed the products that were not fresh. Most of the stale bread was sold at deeply discounted prices through

450 thrift stores operated by the company. The thrift shops were an unprofitable burden on the company but were necessary.

I became interested in Interstate in the fall of 1985 when a friend mentioned that Howard Berkowitz purchased 12 percent of the company's outstanding shares, became chairman of the company's board, and hired a new CEO, who was convinced that he could materially improve the company's profits. I knew Howard Berkowitz and believed that he was a particularly experienced and astute investor. Howard was a founding partner in 1967 of one of the earliest and most successful hedge funds: Steinhardt, Fine, Berkowitz & Co. By the mid-1980s, Howard had left Steinhardt, Fine, Berkowitz and had formed a new hedge fund: HPB Associates. In my opinion, Howard was motivated, caring, and completely honest. I reasoned that Howard would not risk his own money and reputation on Interstate Bakeries unless he was quite confident that his investment would be a success. That is why I became interested in the company's shares.

I knew that the bakery business is a miserable business—among the worst. Most shoppers do not have a strong preference for one brand of bread over another. White bread pretty much is white bread. Whole wheat bread pretty much is whole wheat bread. This relative lack of brand preference gives stores bargaining power over bakeries. A store can threaten a bakery that, if it cannot purchase bread at a certain price, it will seek another supplier. Thus, stores can play one bakery off against another, and they do. Warren Buffett likes businesses that are protected by moats. There are no moats surrounding the bakery business. There are not even any fences or "beware of dog" signs. Therefore, the prices received by the bakeries often are driven to levels so low that it is difficult for the bakeries to earn a decent profit, if any profit at all. This is a key reason why the bread business is a miserable business.

There are other reasons why most bakeries are a poor business. The Teamsters and other unionized employees have work rules that often prevent management from implementing efficiencies. And some of the unionized workers are participants in multiemployer pension plans that the bakeries have little control over—and that can become unquantifiable and burdensome liabilities to the bakeries. Furthermore, managements not only have difficulties controlling prices and labor, but also controlling raw material costs. The prices of wheat, sugar, and other bread ingredients fluctuate based on perceived supply and demand. And management has no control over the price of the gasoline required to fuel the thousands of delivery vans.

For all these reasons, bakeries usually suffer from relatively low profitability and low cash flows. Moreover, because their cash flows are weak, they often struggle to generate sufficient funds to properly maintain and modernize their facilities. Even a mother would have a hard time loving a bakery.

Howard Berkowitz had become interested in Interstate Bakeries at a time when the company was suffering from legacy problems. In 1979, Interstate had been purchased by a failing computer leasing company named DPF. DPF was in the process of liquidating its leasing operations and wanted to purchase another business to justify its continued existence. Also, DPF had large tax loss carry-forwards that could be used to offset the tax obligations of an acquired company. In 1981, DPF finally exited the leasing business and changed its name to Interstate Bakeries. Saddled with DPF's heavy debt load, the renamed Interstate lacked the financial resources to properly modernize and maintain its facilities. Furthermore, management lost focus on the bread business during the years it had to concentrate on unwinding the leasing business. Interstate's profits slipped badly in the early 1980s, and the company was unprofitable in 1984. One of Howard Berkowitz's first actions after becoming chairman of Interstate in 1984 was to replace the existing CEO with Bob Hatch, who had been an executive vice president at General Mills. Bob Hatch quickly announced plans to reduce Interstate's debt and improve its profitability by divesting inefficient plants, optimizing the routing of deliveries, and instituting general cost cutting and efficiencies.

In the fall of 1985, when I decided to analyze Interstate, its shares were selling at about $15. I almost always start my analysis of a company by studying its balance sheet. It is said that a shareholder makes money off the income statement, but survives off the balance sheet, and I agree. Because of my keen desire to survive by minimizing risks of permanent loss, the balance sheet then becomes a good place to start efforts to understand a company. When studying a balance sheet, I look for signs of financial and accounting strengths. Debt-to-equity ratios, liquidity, depreciation rates, accounting practices, pension and health care liabilities, and "hidden" assets and liabilities all are among common considerations, with their relative importance depending on the situation. If I find fault with a company's balance sheet, especially with the level of debt relative to the assets or cash flows, I will abort our analysis, unless there is a compelling reason to do otherwise. In the case of Interstate, Bob Hatch appeared to have performed an excellent job reducing the company's debt and otherwise strengthening its balance sheet. Net debt had declined by $25 million in the company's fiscal year that ended on May 31, 1985, and was continuing to decline in fiscal 1986. I projected that, on May 31, 1986, the company would have only $25 to $28 million of debt versus $85 to $88 million of shareholders' equity. Most other aspects of Interstate's balance sheet also appeared to be in good shape. I was concerned about one potential liability that was not on the balance sheet: potential future liabilities to the multiemployer pension plans. But because the stock market had been strong in recent years, one could reasonably conclude that the asset values of the plans had appreciated sharply and therefore that they would not be a material liability to Interstate in the near future.

If a company's balance sheet passes muster, I then try to get a handle on management. The competence, motivation, and character of management often are critical to the success or failure of a company. To form an opinion on management, I normally pay careful attention to the management's general reputation, read what the management has said in the past, assess whether the management's stated strategies and goals make sense, and analyze whether the management has been successful carrying out its strategies and meeting its goals. However, I am humble about my abilities to accurately assess managements. Experience shows that investors can be unduly impressed by executives who are charismatic or who purposely say what investors want to hear—who play to their audience. Also, investors frequently will undeservedly credit management for a company's favorable results and vice versa. Favorable or unfavorable results often are fortuitous or unfortuitous. A number of years ago, I was one of a few hundred securities analysts attending a particularly charismatic Wall Street presentation by Dennis Kozlowski, the CEO of Tyco International. At the end of the presentation, the audience burst into applause, and one attendee turned to me and said: "Kozlowski might be the single best executive in the country today." A few years later, Tyco was near bankruptcy and Dennis Kozlowski was headed for prison. This is just one example of why one should be humble about his abilities to judge a management. With respect to Interstate Bakeries, I had confidence that Howard Berkowitz had the ability and motivation to select a strong management, and I was impressed by what Bob Hatch had quickly accomplished to improve the company's efficiency and balance sheet.

After trying to get a handle on a company's balance sheet and management, we usually start studying the company's business fundamentals. We try to understand the key forces at work, including (but not limited to) quality of products and services, reputation, competition and protection from future competition, technological and other possible changes, cost structure, growth opportunities, pricing power, dependence on the economy, degree of governmental regulation, capital intensity, and return on capital. Because we believe that information reduces uncertainty, we try to gather as much information as possible. We read and think—and we sometimes speak to customers, competitors, and suppliers. While we do interview the managements of the companies we analyze, we are wary that their opinions and projections will be biased. From experience, we have learned that you should never ask your barber if you need a haircut. In the case of Interstate, it did not take much work to conclude that that the baking business was a lousy business—a particularly lousy business.

It is usually difficult to analyze large quantities of information without the benefit of an insight on how to proceed with the analysis. The insight permits us to separate the information that is critical for decision making from the information that is of secondary or tertiary importance. Once we have determined what is critical, we can start forming opinions and estimating earnings and cash flows. In the case of Interstate Bakeries, I isolated five fundamentals and estimates that appeared critical to our analysis of the company: (1) the balance sheet was OK; (2) management seemed competent and motivated; (3) the business was low-margined and otherwise unattractive; (4) as a best guess, revenues might grow at a 5 percent average annual rate; and (5) a projection by Bob Hatch that pretax margins could increase to 3.5 percent within a few years seemed credible. I note that, whenever we make estimates, we fully realize the impossibility of projecting the future with any certainty. Investing is probabilistic.

When analyzing a company, we almost always build a model of the company's past, present, and projected earnings. Model building helps us structure our thinking and helps us analyze the importance of key variables. Our models normally include earnings projections for the next two or three years.

Once we complete building an earnings model, we usually have sufficient information to value a company. Normally, our valuation is based on a multiple of projected earnings and cash flows. The multiple, in turn, is a function of a company's estimated strengths and projected growth. Over the 50-year period 1960 to 2010, the stock market, as measured by the S&P 500 Index, sold at an average price-to-earnings (PE) ratio of 15.8. Therefore, when valuing companies, I simply use a 15.8 PE ratio for companies of average quality and growth potential, a PE ratio below 15.8 for companies of below-average quality and growth potential, and, of course, a PE ratio above 15.8 for companies of above-average quality and growth potential. It is often difficult to accurately value a company. However, my experience is that a knowledgeable and experienced investor who possesses good judgment can value most companies with sufficient accuracy that he can successfully base his investment decisions on the valuations. Valuations can be directional.

My Excel model for Interstate estimated that the company would earn $2.30 per share in its fiscal year 1988. My assumptions behind the estimate were that revenues would grow at a 5 percent annual rate to $775 million, that pre-tax profit margins would be 3.5 percent, that the effective tax rate would be 30 percent, and that the diluted share count would be 8.2 million.

When valuing Interstate, my conclusions were that its longer-term business fundamentals were unfavorable, its management was good and motivated, and its projected growth rate was somewhat below average. On balance, I valued the company at 11 times earnings. Therefore, I concluded that, two years hence, Interstate's shares would be worth about $25, or about 66 percent above their existing price of $15.

After completing my valuation, my first reaction was that Interstate's shares were not sufficiently inexpensive enough to purchase given the unattractiveness of the business. However, I then had second thoughts. Howard Berkowitz had made a major investment in the company, and he was a knowledgeable gem. I like to follow sound and successful investors who are particularly knowledgeable about a company or industry they are investing in. Also, between mid-1982 and October 1985, the S&P 500 Index had risen by about 68 percent from about 110 to about 185. In October 1985, most stocks were relatively expensive, and I was having difficulty filling our portfolios with stocks that appeared to be more attractive than Interstate's. I find that, in the stock market, it is best to be flexible and not be tied to conventions or rules. Sometimes, it is best to follow your intuitions—and in the case of Interstate, my intuition was that we should own the shares. Over the next few months, I purchased about 8 percent of the outstanding shares of Interstate Bakeries at an average cost of roughly $15 per share.

I note that the processes we use to value stocks and make investment decisions may appear to be ordered, but, in fact, they are quite messy. We constantly are faced with incomplete information, conflicting information, negatives that have to be weighed against positives, and important variables (such as technological change or economic growth) that are difficult to assess and predict. While some of our analysis is quantitative (such as a company's debt-to-equity ratio or a product's share of market), much of it is judgmental. And we need to decide when to cease our analysis and make decisions. In addition, we constantly need to be open to new information that may cause us to alter previous opinions or decisions. It has been said that, if anyone thinks he has a formula for analyzing common stocks, he does not understand how to analyze common stocks.

During the summer of 1986, Howard Berkowitz invited me to join Interstate's board as an ally of his interests. I accepted. My first board meeting on October 15 was a sketch. The meeting was held near the company's headquarters in Kansas City. About a dozen brown-nosing executives approached me, introduced themselves, welcomed me, and commented that they were happy to have me on the board. I didn't know why they were happy to have me on the board. They had never met me before; they did not have my resume; they did not know the first thing about me. One executive, the head of marketing, handed me two enormous garbage bags filled with samples of the company's products. Interstate made dozens of different types of breads sold under various labels and dozens of different types of snack cakes sold under the Dolly Madison and other brand names, and I was gifted a sample of each of them. It was all I could do to lug the huge garbage bags around for the rest of the day and then stuff them into a taxi for the ride back to Kansas City International Airport. The real problem came at the airport. I could not check the garbage bags with the luggage, so I had to carry them aboard the airplane and try to fit them into the overhead storage compartments. They did not come close to fitting. I pushed and pushed and squeezed and squeezed, but to no avail. I then starting removing individual loaves of breads and packages of cakes from the garbage bags and positioning the loaves and cakes in between other passengers' carry-ons, laptops, raincoats, umbrellas, hats, and whatnots. The airplane's pilot announced that the plane could not leave the gate until all passengers were seated with their seat belts fastened. I was standing with my seat belt unfastened and with a loaf of Butternut Light Wholesome Rye Bread in my left hand and a loaf of Butternut Enriched Thinly Sliced Sandwich Bread in my right hand. Another passenger and a flight attendant tried to come to my rescue, while other passengers simply gave me dirty or quizzical looks. I became an unwanted center of attention. Passengers were shaking their heads in disbelief that a man in a formal dark pin-striped suit with a red tie was lugging about 25 loaves of bread and dozens of boxes of donuts and cakes from Kansas City to New York—in garbage bags. Just as I was about to close one of the overhead compartments, a loaf of Millbrook Enriched Pumpernickel Bread lost its balance and landed on a lady's head. Then a bag of Dolly Madison Powdered Donuts landed on another lady's lap. I apologized and told the second lady she could keep the donuts. She looked at me as if I were crazy. And I felt crazy.

When I arrived home late that night, I deposited the garbage bags in the kitchen and went to bed—exhausted more from garbage bags than from the board meeting. The next morning, I could hardly wait to show my wife, Sue, the wide variety of exciting products made by the company I had just become a director of. I displayed the breads and cakes on our kitchen countertops, which they consumed. I thought that their carefully designed packaging brought credit to our kitchen. But Sue thought otherwise. She was aghast when she read the ingredients listed on the labels: "partially hydrogenated animal shortening, cellulose gum, folic acid, sorbic acid, thiamine mononitrate, artificial colors, artificial flavoring, sulfur dioxide." Sue turned to me: "You studied chemistry. Do you know what thiamine mononitrate is? It sounds awful. It sounds like an explosive." I had to admit that in spite of spending hundreds and hundreds of hours in the chemistry laboratories of New Rochelle High School and MIT, and in spite of being a contestant in the Westinghouse Science Talent Search, I did not have the foggiest notion what thiamine mononitrate was. But the name did sound awful—and the names of many of the other ingredients sounded even worse than awful. So when my wife said that the breads and cakes and donuts had to "go immediately," I quickly agreed. Anyway, it would have taken us months to consume all the products, and they would have totally devastated our waistlines. I suggested that we donate the breads and cakes to a soup kitchen, but Sue immediately nixed the suggestion: "Laden with all those chemicals, they are not fit for anyone." So, the 25 or so loaves of bread and the dozens of varieties of sugary sweet cakes and donuts went back into their garbage bags and were deposited with the garbage.

We completely lucked out with our investment in Interstate Bakeries. Between early 1986 and mid-summer 1986, the price of wheat fell from about $3.20 per bushel to as low as $2.25 in reaction to prospects for a large crop. Also, between the fall of 1985 and mid-summer 1986, the price of crude oil collapsed from close to $30 per barrel to about $10. Because Interstate consumed large quantities of wheat and gasoline (for its delivery trucks), the sharp declines in the prices of wheat and crude oil were major cost savings for the company. When the prices of raw materials decline, competition usually forces companies to pass on most of the cost savings to their customers, but with a lag. In the case of Interstate Bakeries, the cost savings were so large and the lag in price reductions was sufficiently long that the company's profits increased sharply. In the fiscal year that ended on May 31, 1986, Interstate's pretax profits before restructuring charges were $14.6 million. A year later, the comparable number was $20.7 million. While a portion of the 42 percent increase in earnings should be credited to management's successful efforts to reduce costs, the largest percentage by far was due to the sharp decline in the cost of wheat and gasoline.

In February 1987, Howard Berkowitz wisely decided that it was a good time to take advantage of the large increase in profits by selling the company. The board of directors readily agreed and retained Goldman Sachs to value Interstate and to advise on how it should be sold. On March 27, Goldman told a committee of the board that, if the company was auctioned, its shares might be worth $32 to $35 if the purchaser was not in the baking business and might be worth up to $40 if the purchaser was a baker that could achieve strategic or synergistic benefits and eliminate a competitor. My original valuation had been $25 per share. Thus, I was smiling.

In the spring of 1987, Goldman Sachs prepared a selling brochure and contacted possible purchasers. In the meanwhile, Bob Hatch, who likely would have lost his job if Interstate was acquired by a competitor, contacted First Boston Corporation and suggested that First Boston and he should form a group to purchase control of the company. First Boston agreed. On June 6, the Hatch–First Boston group offered to purchase all the shares owned by the largest shareholders for $35 per share. The purchase would have given the group effective control of the company. After the Interstate board turned down the Hatch–First Boston bid, Bob Hatch told the board that it was a poor time to sell the company and suggested that the board terminate its efforts to sell. However, Howard Berkowitz held the chips—and Howard wanted to realize his profits at a time when the company's profits seemed to be temporarily inflated.

Efforts to sell the company proceeded. Eleven parties showed a preliminary interest in acquiring Interstate, and four eventually demonstrated sufficient interest that they were willing to sign confidentiality agreements that allowed full access to all of the company's confidential financial and operating data. The Hatch–First Boston group was one of the four parties. All the other three were other baking companies. By showing interest in acquiring Interstate, a competitor could obtain a free look at Interstate's confidential books. Thus, a competitor would be foolish if it did not show interest in acquiring Interstate, whether the interest was serious or feigned.

On August 11, Interstate issued a press release stating that it had received informal indications of interest in acquiring the company. In response to the release, the price of Interstate's shares jumped from $28.875 to $36.25.

Interstate's board was concerned that the Hatch–First Boston group would be the only party seriously interested in purchasing the company and that the three competitor bakeries were only feigning serious interest. Therefore, it was decided that there would be a closed auction for the company. Bids would be submitted in sealed envelopes. At 5:00 p.m. on Friday, September 11, the envelopes would be opened. The winning bidder would be required to sign a definitive purchase contract almost immediately after its bid was accepted because the board was worried that, if the Hatch–First Boston group learned that it had been the only bidder, it would renege on its bid.

When the envelopes were opened by Goldman Sachs, Hatch–First Boston was the winning bidder at $38 per share. Hatch–First Boston was the only bidder. Goldman Sachs conferred with the board and it was decided to tell Hatch–First Boston that they could own the company if they increased their bid to $40.50. That took nerves. Huge nerves. At about 11:00 a.m. on the 12th, Hatch–First Boston agreed to the $40.50 price, and a few hours later a definitive purchase contract was signed.

Interstate's board met on Sunday, September 13, to approve the transaction. Most of the meeting was conducted by Paul Roth of Schulte Roth & Zabel, the company's legal counsel for the transaction. Paul read the riot act. It was the legal responsibility of the board to consider all offers for the company and all other alternatives. Before agreeing to the acquisition, the board had to make 100 percent certain that the transaction was the best available option for the company's shareholders. Otherwise, the board would be guilty of woeful neglect or much worse. The discussion and analysis of the alternatives then commenced. I have a type AA personality, and after about two tedious hours of debate on whether Hatch–First Boston's amazingly and unwisely high bid was in the best interest of the shareholders, I lost patience and blurted out: "You don't have to step on a scale to know you are fat, and this board has been weighing the Hatch–First Boston bid for two long hours on a scale that continually measures that the bid is so fat that it is in danger of breaking the scale. So let's approve the transaction and go back to our wives and children." Paul Roth gave me a dirty look and stated that I evidently had not been listening to his description of the legal responsibilities of the board. The discussion and analysis then continued for another few tedious and seemingly unnecessary hours before the board formally approved the transaction.

The saga of the acquisition of Interstate was not complete on September 13. On October 19, the stock market fell apart. The S&P 500 Index declined by 20.9 percent during the day. I was concerned that Hatch–First Boston, now aware that they were the only bidder and aware that they were overpaying for a miserable business, would claim force majeure, and would try to wheedle out of the acquisition. Indeed, Hatch–First Boston did try to cancel the deal, but the purchase contract had been so tightly written by Paul Roth that there were almost no outs. On Monday, October 26, the acquisition was completed.

There is a postscript. The Hatch–First Boston group brought Interstate public again in 1991 and used the proceeds from the offering to reduce the company's debt. Then, in 1995, Interstate acquired Continental Baking, a troubled subsidiary of Ralston Purina, for $330 million in cash plus 16.9 million newly issued Interstate shares. Five years later, Interstate repurchased 15.5 million of the 16.9 million shares held by Ralston Purina for $244 million. It appears that the repurchase was Interstate's undoing. The repurchase increased Interstate's debt by $244 million and reduced its tangible book value by a like amount. On May 31, 2001, Interstate had net debt of $595 million and a tangible book value of minus $20 million—which, of course, is a totally precarious balance sheet. The totally precarious balance sheet led to disaster three years later, when operating losses triggered a violation in the company's bond indentures. The company was in deep financial trouble. On September 22, 2004, Interstate filed for bankruptcy under Chapter 11. It did not emerge from bankruptcy until 2009, and then was forced to refile under Chapter 11 in early 2012, partially because of large pension obligations to multiemployer union plans and partially because of inefficiencies stemming from restrictive work rules. In November 2012, the company announced that it could not continue as a going enterprise and intended to liquidate, selling off its various brands to the highest bidders. Interstate Bakeries had been a melting ice cube that had completely melted.

There are some lessons to be learned from Interstate Bakeries. While the company's shares were not deeply undervalued relative to the quality of the company, I decided to place a sizable bet on the shares because its chairman was particularly capable and was highly incentivized to act in the interest of the shareholders. The bet paid off. When Interstate's earnings surged due to sharply lower costs for wheat and gasoline, Howard Berkowitz was astute enough to realize that the surge likely was transitory. And because he owned 924,800 of the company's shares, he was highly incentivized financially to put the company up for sale.

Bob Hatch, however, owned relatively few shares. In my opinion, his primary incentive was to maintain his position as CEO. As CEO, he earned more than $500,000 per year and enjoyed substantial perks and prestige. What role did Bob Hatch's personal interests play in his initial opinion that the company should not be sold? What role did his interests play in the high price that Hatch–First Boston bid for the company, a winning bid that permitted Bob Hatch to remain CEO, but a bid that must have been based on considerable wishful thinking?

I do not have definitive answers to these questions, but I do believe that managements and investors tend to act in their own self-interest—and I strongly suspect that Interstate Bakeries is a case in point.

Another lesson is that too much debt can be fatal. My father-in-law advised me to invest cautiously so that, under arduous circumstances, we would survive and "live for another day." When Interstate's management highly leveraged the company by repurchasing $244 million of its shares, it jeopardized the financial viability of the company. As a result, Interstate Bakeries was not able to live for another day. I turn down many otherwise attractive investments because of their weak balance sheets, and I believe that this discipline is a material reason for our success over the years.

5

U.S. HOME CORPORATION

I frequently use Bloomberg's data banks to run screens. I screen for companies that are selling at low price-to-earnings (PE) ratios, low prices to revenues, low price-to-book values, or low prices relative to other relevant metrics. Usually, the screens produce a number of stocks that merit additional analyses, but almost always the additional analyses conclude that there are valid reasons for the apparent undervaluations. During my career, I probably have run thousands of screens, but only a tiny fraction of 1 percent have resulted in a successful investment idea. Using screens to find investment ideas is like searching for a single pin in a field of haystacks.

In mid-1994, while screening for companies selling at large discounts to their book values, I came across the name U.S. Home, a builder of single-family homes. My early read showed that the company had entered Chapter 11 bankruptcy in 1991 and had emerged from Chapter 11 in 1993 as a profitable company with an average-quality balance sheet for a homebuilder. The company had a book value of about $27 per share and was earning about $2.50 per share. The shares were selling at about $17, or at only about 0.63 times book and 6.8 times earnings. Very low multiples of book and earnings are adrenaline flows for value investors. I eagerly decided to investigate further.

I noticed that the law firm of Kaye Scholer had represented U.S. Home in its bankruptcy proceedings. I knew the managing partner of Kaye Scholer and gave him a call. It was a lucky call. The managing partner was very familiar with U.S. Home and its management. In Kaye Scholer's opinion, U.S. Home had entered bankruptcy because of a weak housing market in Texas in the mid-1980s, followed by a general recession in the housing market in 1990. The company had been overexposed to the Texas housing market at a time when a sudden sharp decline in the price of crude oil led to a weak demand for new homes in oil-centric areas of Texas. Within a few months, demand turned so soft that U.S. Home was forced to close 36 of the 70 subdivisions it was operating in the Houston area. The soft market in the mid-1980s weakened the company's financial strength—and then the housing recession in 1990 served as a knockout punch. Importantly, according to my friend at Kaye Scholer, U.S. Home's financial problems had been created by external problems and, except for its finances, the company had been well managed, efficient, and highly regarded.

I immediately developed the thesis that U.S. Home's shares were undeservedly depressed because of the stigma of the bankruptcy. I reasoned that, with time, the stigma would diminish and the shares would appreciate. I then started to learn more about the company and its industry.

U.S. Home was formed in 1959 upon the merger of several small homebuilders. The company grew organically and by acquisition and, by the mid-1980s, had revenues in excess of $1 billion. The company seemed to enjoy a good reputation for producing quality homes, and it seemed to be growing. Its net debt was somewhat high, but the debt was backed by inventories of raw land, developed lots, and homes under construction. There was nothing wrong with the company, but there was nothing to write home about it.

Homebuilding seemed to be an industry of average quality and average growth potential. The business works as follows. Homebuilders normally purchase large tracts of undeveloped land. They then seek permits from local authorities to subdivide and develop the land. Development includes the construction of roads and the laying of water, sewage, natural gas, and electrical lines. Then, homebuilders normally build a few model homes and open the subdivision for business. While the models and some other houses in a subdivision are built before they are sold, most homes are not built until a sales contract is received and a deposit is paid. After a house is completed, a certificate of occupancy is received, and title then passes to the purchaser.

Historically, most single-family homes were built by local builders. Eventually, some of the local builders became larger, expanded geographically, and became publicly owned. The larger publicly owned companies enjoy efficiencies of scale and, importantly, access to the capital markets. The access generally gives the public companies an advantage when borrowing to finance the purchase of raw land, the development of lots, and the construction of homes.

I studied U.S. Home's financial statements, constructed an earnings model, and concluded that the company could earn $3 to $4 per share by 1996 or 1997. Initially, I valued the company at about 12 times earnings, and therefore believed that the shares would be worth $36 to $48 two or three years down the road. However, I noticed that other builders typically sold for somewhat less than 12 times earnings. For some reason, the homebuilding industry was not highly regarded on Wall Street. In fact, the industry earned the pejorative nickname "stick builders." Therefore, I toned down my expectations. However, even if U.S. Home's shares were worth only 10 times earnings, they appeared to be an attractive investment opportunity given that they were selling at only $17 at the time. So, I started buying the shares.

It turned out that U.S. Home was a frustrating holding. The company itself did fine, much better than I expected. Between 1994 and 1999, the company's revenues increased by 91 percent, and its earnings more than doubled from $2.50 per share to $5.30 per share. Given these results, the shares should have been an out-of-the-park home run. But they were not.

The shares continued to sell at 6 to 7 times earnings. Management tried to promote interest in the shares. Bob Strudler, the company's chairman, told U.S Home's story to anyone who would listen. On March 5, 1997, the company held a full-day meeting for securities analysts. I thought Bob Strudler did an excellent job explaining the company's strategies, strengths, and growth potentials, but to no avail. In June, the shares sold at a lower price than they had sold at in early March.

In 1998 and 1999, I spoke to Bob Strudler frequently. Usually when I speak to an executive of a company, my questions are honed in on the fundamentals of the company—on new products, competition, strategies, and finances. But my conversations with Bob were centered on why his stock sold at 6 to 7 times earnings and at a material discount to its book value. We both were perplexed. U.S. Home was a well-managed, successful company. Almost no decent company sold at 6 to 7 times earnings and at a discount to book value. U.S. Home was a value investor's dream. I recommended the stock to a number of other money managers. The shares continued to sell at 6 to 7 times earnings. I was more than frustrated.

Finally, in early 2000, somebody else recognized that U.S Home was selling at a bargain price. The somebody was another homebuilder, Lennar Corporation. Lennar acquired (really "stole") U.S. Home for $34¾, or for only 6.6 times earnings. Usually, when a company bids to acquire one of our holdings, we have cause to celebrate. Champagne corks pop. But I had no cause to celebrate receiving 6.6 times earnings for U.S. Home's shares. We had owned the shares for about six years and had about doubled our money. That works out to an average annual return of about 12 percent. Since our goal is to achieve average annual returns of 15 to 20 percent (and hopefully closer to 20 percent than 15 percent), the investment was not successful.

However, there is a bright side to the story. Ownership of U.S. Homes' shares led us to one of the most profitable investment ideas in our history—to a home run. The home run is the subject of the next chapter.

6

CENTEX CORPORATION

In the late 1990s, U.S. Home's revenues were growing faster than I had projected, and the company was gaining market share. For example, in 1999 the company sold 12.0 percent more homes than in 1998, while the total number of housing units built in the United States increased by only 1.5 percent. My curiosity was aroused, so I checked the recent growth rates of other publicly owned homebuilders. They also were growing much faster than their industry. What was going on? If the public homebuilders were growing faster than their industry, then the private homebuilders must be lagging. Why were they lagging? I picked up the phone and called a friend who built a few homes each year in lower Westchester County. My friend thought that my inquiry was ill informed—in fact, dumb: hadn't I ever heard of the S&L crisis?

In the 1980s, savings and loan banks (commonly known as S&Ls or thrifts) were badly squeezed by high interest rates. Many of the mortgages that the S&Ls issued in the 1960s and 1970s were at fixed and relatively low interest rates. Then, in the late 1970s and in the early 1980s, interest rates increased sharply. To attract the requisite level of deposits, the S&Ls were forced to pay high interest rates on deposits. As a result, their net interest margins often were insufficient to cover their overhead expenses. Furthermore, when the real estate market softened in 1990, many of the loans issued by the S&Ls went into default. The S&Ls were in deep trouble. Many declared bankruptcy and closed. Others were forced to merge. The crisis became so severe that the Federal Savings and Loan Insurance Corporation, which had been established by an act of Congress in 1934, had to be abolished because it became too insolvent to save.

Historically, the S&Ls and community banks provided the bulk of the financing needed by small homebuilders to purchase land, develop land, and construct houses. During the housing recession of 1990, many small homebuilders suffered operating losses and could not repay their loans. As a result, most of the S&Ls and banks that did survive the crisis were less eager to lend to small builders. With less financing available and with tightened lending standards, many small homebuilders lacked sufficient capital to build nearly as many homes as they had built previously. Some small builders decided to finish existing projects and then retire. Others decided to build at reduced rates. Between 1990 and 2000, the number of homes built by small builders continually and materially declined. The vacuum was filled by the publicly owned homebuilders. This explains why the large builders were growing at a much faster rate than their market.

I quickly calculated the growth rates of several large builders. In 1999, Centex built 27 percent more homes than in 1998.[1] Comparable growth rates for Pulte and Lennar were 20 percent and 17 percent. Something was happening that was big. Stick building had become a growth industry. Stick builders were growing as rapidly as most Internet companies. I made a model of Centex's earnings. I assumed that, for the next several years, the company sold 12 percent more homes each year and that the average price per home increased at a 2 percent annual rate. Next, I looked at profit margins. Centex's pretax earnings in 1999 equaled 8.1 percent of sales. Surely, if the company's revenues increased at a 14 percent annual rate, its profit margins would benefit from positive leverage over fixed costs. After studying some historical numbers, I estimated that Centex's pretax margins would reach 10 percent by 2003. Thus, my model estimated that the company's revenues would increase from $6,008 million in 1999 to $10,150 million in 2003 and that its pretax earnings would increase from $482 million to $1,015 million. After taxes at a 35 percent effective rate and based on a share count of 125 million, my model projected 2003 after-tax earnings at $5.25 per share. Because the homebuilding industry was becoming a growth industry (I would no longer call the companies "stick builders"), I valued Centex at 12 times earnings. Therefore, I estimated that the shares would be worth about $63 in 2003. At the time I reached this conclusion, the shares were selling at less than $12. I did not wait a minute. I immediately started checking my thesis with anybody who had knowledge of the homebuilding industry and who would listen. I did not learn anything from my checking that would cause me to change my model. I then read Wall Street reports on the industry. I could not find a single Wall Street report that concluded that the public homebuilders would enjoy accelerated growth at the expense of the private homebuilders. Thus, it appeared that others were not on to my idea. I was gaining confidence that the homebuilders were an unusually attractive investment opportunity. I was literally jumping up and down with excitement. I could not wait, and immediately started purchasing shares of Centex and several other homebuilders.

I faced the question of how many shares of Centex and other homebuilders to purchase. There is no single correct answer to the optimum diversity in a portfolio. My own policy is that no single stock should equal more than 12 percent of the total value of a portfolio and that no single industry should equal more than 25 percent of the total value. When measuring the percentages, I use the cost of the stock rather than its market price. That way, I am not forced to reduce the size of a position that appreciates faster than the portfolio as a whole.

Our concept that the large homebuilders would grow rapidly at the expense of the small homebuilders was a creative idea. Because I have been interested in how we can optimize our creativity, over the years I have tried to learn how others successfully generate original ideas. I have yet to find an answer, but I did find that the following excerpts from an analysis by Professor Robert Harris were helpful:

Creativity is the ability to generate new ideas by combining, changing, or reapplying existing ideas.

Very few works of creative excellence are produced with a single stroke of brilliance or in a frenzy of rapid activity.

Creativity is also an attitude: the ability to accept change and newness—a willingness to play with ideas and possibilities, a flexibility of outlook, the habit of enjoying the good, while looking for ways to improve it. Creative people usually do not have a need to conform and are not afraid of failure.[2]

It is difficult to find creative investment ideas. Thinking is hard work. Most investment ideas that run through one's head already have run through the heads of others, and therefore likely already have been largely discounted into the prices of stocks. If you have reason to believe that the price of oil will increase sharply, but if the likelihood of sharply higher oil prices already has become the conventional wisdom among investors, then it probably is too late to purchase the shares of companies that own oil reserves. Morning after morning, lunch after lunch, afternoon after afternoon, I try to find new creative investment ideas—but the vast majority of the time I strike out. Thus, my research efforts usually are tedious and frustrating. I have hundreds of thoughts and I study hundreds of companies, but good investment ideas are few and far between. Maybe only 1 percent or so of the companies we study ends up being part of our portfolios—making it much harder for a stock to enter our portfolios than for a student to enter Harvard. However, when I do find an exciting idea, excitement fills the air—a blaze of light that more than compensates for the hours and hours of tedium and frustration.

Our idea that the publicly owned homebuilders would enjoy materially accelerated growth is consistent with Professor Harris's analysis. We generated the new idea by observing trends in an old idea (U.S. Home). We were unwilling to conform to Wall Street's general view that stick building was a relatively unattractive cyclical business. We were not afraid of failure.

By mid-2000, we had built a large position in Centex and a few other homebuilders. Centex was by far the largest of the holdings, largely because I was particularly impressed by the company's CEO, Larry Hirsch, and by the company's general reputation for quality. Now, we just had to monitor our holdings, try to relax, and wait to see if our analyses and projections would prove to be accurate. I note that we are most relaxed at the times when we purchase a security and when we sell a security, but it is often difficult to relax in between. There is a reason for this. Greenhaven's goal is to achieve average annual returns of 15 to 20 percent on its investments. Because we make mistakes, to achieve 15 to 20 percent average returns, we usually do not purchase a security unless we believe that it has the potential to provide a 30 percent or so annual return. Thus, we have very high expectations for each investment. After we purchase a security, there are two possibilities. The unlikely possibility is that the security starts appreciating at above a 30 percent or so annual rate, in which case we are relaxed and smiling. The more likely possibility is that the security fails to appreciate at a 30 percent or so annual rate, in which case we are disappointed and unrelaxed.

There is another consideration. We are prone to sell securities that have exceeded our expectations and hold securities that have yet to meet our expectations. Thus, at any one time, because we have sold our winners, our portfolio is heavily weighted toward stocks that have lagged our expectations. Owning laggards is neither fun nor relaxing.

Because the homebuilders had become a sizable investment, over the next several years, we continually and particularly carefully monitored the progress of the companies. I was generally happy that the large homebuilders continued to gain market share. Centex sold 61 percent more homes in 2003 than in 1999. Furthermore, Centex's pretax margins had increased to 11.1 percent and its earnings per share had increased to $6.01 in 2003 versus $2.11 in 1999. Responding to the sharply higher earnings, the price of the company's shares had appreciated to about $40, more than three times the price we had paid for the shares three years earlier. However, the shares still were selling at far less than 10 times earnings, which was a frustrating disappointment—and an enigma.

On a warm and humid day in mid-July 2003, I found a number that intrigued me. The U.S. Census Bureau keeps track of the number of housing units being built in the United States. On the twelfth business day of each month, the Bureau releases data for the previous month. The data for June showed that the seasonally adjusted annual rate of housing starts during the month was 1,867,000, up 6.7 percent from May and up 8.7 percent from the previous June. Those are large increases for an industry that should only grow in line with the growth of the U.S. population. Something was going on. I needed to find out what. The answer seemed to lie with the economy and mortgage rates. In the late 1990s, there was a boom in the prices of technology stocks. In fact, the boom developed into a bubble. The increased wealth created by the boom contributed to a strengthened economy. In turn, the strengthened economy triggered an increase in interest rates. Thirty-year fixed mortgage rates increased from about 7 percent in 1997 to about 8 percent in 2000. Then, the technology bubble burst and the economy softened. Thirty-year fixed mortgage rates declined to about 7 percent by early 2001. The terrorist attacks on 9/11 were a second and severe blow to the economy. Immediately following the attacks, many Americans were not in the mood to travel or to purchase large-ticket items. Responding to the weak economy, the Federal Reserve Bank sharply reduced interest rates. Ninety-day T-bill rates fell from about 3.5 percent just before the attacks to about 1.7 percent by year-end 2011. 30-year fixed rate mortgages fell from about 7 percent before the attacks to just over 6 percent a year later and then to about 5.2 percent by mid-2003. With mortgage rates at 5.2 percent, the purchase of a new house was more affordable than it had been for quite a while. Many families decided to take advantage of the affordability, which was the apparent reason why the demand for new houses had increased to above-normal levels.

The number of houses that can be built at any one time is limited by the availability of permitted and developed building lots. Because of local opposition, it often requires several years to receive permits to develop raw land. Opposition due to environmental impacts often is particularly sticky. I once read about a proposed housing development that was delayed several years because of local concerns about the well-being of a family of frogs that reputedly lived in a stream that crossed the property. My kidding and impolitic solution to the concerns and delays was sautéed frog legs, but the local conservationists evidently did not care for frog legs, and they dragged their opposition into the courts.

Because of the time required to permit and develop land, by mid-2003 the demand for new homes was increasing faster than building lots could be permitted and developed. The result was a shortage of new homes in many parts of the country. When a new housing development finally was ready to accept orders, often there were many more hopeful purchasers than available homes. Long lines developed in front of the selling offices. To be near the front of a line, some families camped out at the development for one or more nights. With demand exceeding supply, housing prices started to increase at above normal rates. Newspapers started carrying articles about the price increases. Many newspaper journalists and economists predicted that housing prices would continue to increase quite sharply for the foreseeable future. These predictions incentivized additional families to purchase new homes before prices did increase further. Hence, the boom fed on itself. By the fall of 2003, seasonally adjusted housing starts reached an annual rate of 2 million—and likely would have been higher had there been a greater availability of developed lots.

It may seem counterintuitive, but I was unhappy about the sudden boom in single-family houses. We believed that the normal annual demand for new housing units in the United States was about 1,600,000. Over time, the average annual demand is relatively fixed because there are only a certain number of people living in the United States who need a home. A recalcitrant wayward teenager who hates his parents is unlikely to run away from home and purchase, to quote from an advertisement, a "new perfectly proportioned 4 bedroom, 3.5 bath house with cathedraled ceiling master bedroom; large beautifully landscaped 0.8 acre yard contiguous to a permanently deeded nature preserve; close to nationally awarded schools and fine shopping." With housing starts at a 2 million annual rate, clearly more houses were being built than needed. Future demand had been pulled forward, first by the attractive affordability and then by the expectation of continually rising prices There may have been some pent-up demand for houses coming out of the 2001–2002 recession, but, sooner or later, if housing construction continued at late 2003 levels, there would be a surplus of unsold homes—and the housing industry would cycle downward. When we purchased Centex and the other homebuilders, we hoped they would grow steadily for many years at double-digit rates as they gained market share. We also hoped that their shares would sell at higher price-to-earnings (PE) ratios as they became viewed as growth stocks rather than cyclical stick builders. However, if the industry cycled downward, we might suffer through a period of declining earnings and declining PE ratios. That is why I was unhappy about the spurt in the demand for new houses.

The housing boom continued through 2004 and 2005. Centex continued to benefit from the boom. The company was projected to sell about 39,000 houses in 2005, up from 30,358 in 2003 and 18,904 in 1999. Furthermore, the company's pretax profit margins in 2005 were expected to exceed 14 percent and the company's earnings per share was projected to equal or exceed $9. Centex was on a roll.

In the fall of 2005, Centex's shares were selling at about $70. We had earned close to a sixfold profit on our investment. I should have been ecstatic, but I was not. The shares still were trading at far less than 10 times earnings. Furthermore, the housing boom could not continue forever, and when it ended, Centex's earnings likely would decline sharply. Also, the company was aggressively purchasing additional land at a time when land prices had risen sharply in response to both strong demand from the homebuilders and limited supply due to frogs and other environmental concerns. At the end of 2004, Centex owned 96,945 building lots, up 25 percent from the end of 2003. To finance these purchases, Centex's net corporate debt increased by more than $500 million in 2004. I thought that the company was making a large and dangerous mistake. At a time when the housing industry was abnormally strong, Centex should have been husbanding its cash and minimizing its purchases of high-priced land. The risks in owing shares in the homebuilders clearly had increased. I started to call them stick builders again, and I started to reduce our holdings.

I badly needed to speak to Centex's management. Larry Hirsch had retired as CEO in 2004 and had been replaced by Tim Eller. I called Tim and arranged an appointment to see him on November 15. I decided to bring along an acquaintance, Jim Grossfeld, who previously had been CEO of Pulte Homes and whom I had met and respected when we both were directors of Interstate Bakeries. The meeting with Tim Eller was stormy. I tried to understand the thinking behind Centex's strategy of paying high prices for land at a time when home construction was at an unsustainably high level. It was clear to me that an excessive number of houses were being built in the United States and eventually there would be a correction that likely would lead to lower prices for houses. If Centex received lower prices on new homes that were sitting on top of high-cost land, the company could suffer serious operating losses and value impairments. Tim did not agree with my reasoning. He maintained that the large homebuilders would continue to gain market share and therefore that Centex would need all the land it was purchasing. He thought it unlikely that housing prices would decline, even during a slowdown. His argument was that house prices never had declined before. I took strong exception to this reasoning. It is dangerous to project past trends into the future. It is akin to steering a car by looking through the rearview mirror (which is OK while the road remains straight, but a catastrophe when the car comes to a curve). We agreed to disagree. I was frustrated. I was angry. My father always told me to slowly count to 10 whenever I was angry, and then the anger would disappear. I counted to 10 very slowly. I was still angry. I counted to 10 again. I remained angry and frustrated. The large homebuilders were gaining market share and were selling at low prices relative to their current earnings, but there were material risks of permanent losses if excessive inventories of unsold homes triggered a downward cycle in the business. Tim Eller seemed oblivious to the risks.

I decided to sell all our holdings in the homebuilders. I could not wait for signs that the demand for new homes was weakening. When purchasing or selling securities, we try to act ahead of developments. We were out of our holdings by early 2006. We sold our Centex shares at roughly $70, or close to 6 times what we had paid for the shares. The investment was a complete winner, but I felt that it could have been even more profitable if the housing bubble had not occurred because the homebuilders eventually would have earned respect and sold at much higher PE ratios.

While I was happy with the outcome of our investments in the home-builders, I was not completely happy or fulfilled. I usually am that way: a happy and optimistic person who, at the same time, is unhappy that he is not doing better. Put it this way: I would be less than happy if I were not constantly striving to do better. A desire and striving to do better seems to be part of human behavior, at least my human behavior.

The housing crisis that followed the bursting of the bubble was worse than I would have imagined. Who is to blame for the crisis? Certainly the banks, Wall Street firms, and mortgage brokers that aggressively oversold risky mortgages are partially to blame. And certainly the homebuilders, who misjudged the fundamentals of their business and overexpanded, are partly to blame. But also to blame are the many families who overpaid for houses—the Tom and Jane Smiths who were not at all interested in purchasing a house at a reasonable price in 2002, but who then camped out and overpaid for a house in 2005 because they believed that prices would continue to rise. According to U.S. Census Bureau data, the average price for a new single-family home increased from $228,700 in 2002 to $292,200 in 2005. Even adjusting for inflation, the Tom and Jane Smiths materially overpaid—and then likely financed their purchases with mort-gages that were larger than the houses would have been worth in 2002—and materially larger than the houses were worth after the bubble burst. No wonder there was a financial crisis. In my opinion, greedy bankers and Wall Streeters contributed to the housing and financial crises, but the fam-ilies who purchased homes in 2004–2006 at inflated prices were the root cause of the crises. Wall Street and banks, of course, became the scapegoats and received nearly full blame for the crisis. It would have been impolitic to criticize the Tom and Jane Smiths for their indiscretions.

Several months after we sold our holdings in Centex and several other homebuilders for happily large gains, I received an unhappy telephone call from Bill Summer, a client who was in the real estate business. Bill complained that, because of the large realized capital gains in the homebuilders, he now was faced with an unhappily large tax bill. He added that he did not like paying taxes to the government and that, in his real estate business, he had found ways to permanently defer paying taxes. He asked me to review his portfolio and sell all his stocks that had unrealized losses so that he could offset the realized gains with losses. I explained to him that we luckily did not have any sizable unrealized losses. Furthermore, if we realized losses in stocks and then repurchased the stocks 31 days later, clients would establish lower cost bases and therefore eventually would realize larger gains when we sold the shares. The larger gains would negate the tax savings of realizing the losses. Greenhaven typically holds stocks for two to four years. Thus, clients who sell shares to take tax losses merely would be deferring realized gains for a few years. And there are some distinct disadvantages to selling attractive stocks for the purpose of realizing losses. There are transactional costs when stocks are purchased and sold. Also, there is an upward bias to the stock market, so, on average, it will cost something not to own a stock for 31 days. Further, and importantly, if a stock is sold and then repurchased, the stock needs to be held for one year and a day from the date of repurchase to be treated as a long-term capital gain. If we desire or need to sell a repurchased stock at a profit within one year of when it was repurchased, any gain on the transaction would be taxed at ordinary rates. Thus, while tax loss selling permits clients to, in effect, borrow money from the government at no cost, I believe that the disadvantages of tax loss selling normally outweigh the advantages—and I told that to Bill.

A few days later, Bill called back, still grumbling about his tax bill. I told him that we were committed to making investment decisions that were in the best interest of our clients and that, while tax loss selling made sense to us a small fraction of the time, it did not make sense to us most of the time. I suggested to Bill that if not paying taxes was a major investment objective, he should leave Greenhaven, which he did.

NOTES

1. Centex's fiscal year ended on March 31. For Centex, when referring to a particular year, I am really referring to the fiscal year that ended on the following March 31.
2. Robert Harris, *Introduction to Creative Thinking*, version date April, 2, 2012; http://www.virtualsalt.com/crebook1.htm

7

UNION PACIFIC (RAILROAD)

Circa 2000 B.C., horses were domesticated and used for transportation. A horse can travel about five miles per hour over moderate distances. For the next 3,800 years, technological innovation for traveling on land was almost nonexistent. In 1800, the horse still was the prime method of transportation on land—and still at about five miles per hour. So 3,800 years of stagnation!

Everything started to change in 1769 when James Watt designed an efficient steam engine. Originally, steam engines were used to power pumps and industrial machinery, but soon inventors saw the potential to use the engines to power boats. While a number of steamboats were built by entrepreneurs as early as 1787, Robert Fulton became known as the father of steam navigation when, on August 7, 1807, his *Clermont* completed the 150-mile trip from New York to Albany in 32 hours—still an average speed of five miles an hour.

If steam engines could be used to power boats, why couldn't they be used to power wagons that ride on tracks? They could. In 1814, a self-educated

British laborer named George Stephenson designed the world's first steam locomotive to operate on tracks. The purpose of the locomotive was to haul coal from the mouth of a mine. Eleven years later, the first common carrier railroad, the Stockton & Darlington Railroad Company, was formed. Stephenson designed a locomotive for the Stockton & Darlington that could pull 6 coal cars and 21 small passenger cars over nine miles of track in about one hour—already nearly twice the speed of a horse.

In the United States, the city of Baltimore decided to build a railroad to Ohio to compete with the Erie Canal, which, at the time, was the least expensive transportation route from the farms in the Midwest. On July 4, 1828, with great fanfare, Charles Carroll, the last surviving signer of the Declaration of Independence, symbolically dug a spade of dirt to commence construction of the Baltimore and Ohio Railroad (B&O). In early 1830, the B&O became America's first commercial railroad when it started operations on 13 miles of completed track. But expansion to Ohio was slow. Bridges had to be built, tunnels dug. In 1868, the B&O finally reached the Ohio River. Then, three years were required to construct a bridge to span the river. At last, in 1871, the railroad reached the farmlands of Ohio.

The almost immediate commercial success of the B&O in the 1830s and 1840s sparked a boom in the construction of railroads. By 1840, about 3,000 miles of track were in operation. By 1860, about 30,000 miles. Between 1815 and 1860, the cost of moving farm produce and manufactured goods over long distances fell by 95 percent. In 1860, trains could average about 20 miles per hour over a 24-hour day. The horse was on the way out for long distance travel. The railroads had revolutionized transportation. They were the Internet of their day.

Soon, the growth and potential profitability of railroads attracted the attention of Cornelius Vanderbilt, Edward Harriman, Jay Gould, and other wealthy businessmen and speculators, who purchased control of many regional railroads in order to create local monopolies that could set high rates (i.e., prices). In 1887, the U.S. Congress, responding to complaints from many farmers and other users of railroads about the high rates, passed the Interstate Commerce Act, which made the railroads subject to federal regulation. The act formed the five-member Interstate Commerce Commission (ICC), which had the power to regulate many aspects of the railroads, including the rates they could charge.

The railroads continued to grow and generally prosper until the 1920s, when the automobile started to erode passenger travel by rail. Then in the 1930s, the railroads suffered heavily during the Great Depression. Their revenues declined by about 50 percent between 1928 and 1933—and by 1937 many were in receivership. At the outset of World War II, the entire railroad industry was in trouble. War-related traffic from 1942 to 1945 brought a reprieve to the industry's stressed condition, but the reprieve was temporary. Soon after the war ended, the construction of the interstate highway system gave trucks a competitive advantage over railroads for many types of cargo. By the mid-1970s, the railroad's share of intercity freight traffic had declined to 35 percent, down from 75 percent in 1930. Usage of railroads to carry passengers also declined sharply after the end of the war, partially due to the construction of the interstate highway system and partially to the commercialization of the jet airplane.

The plight of the railroads was further aggravated by poor and excessive regulation. The ICC established rates. In an effort to help farmers, rates for grains and other bulk farm produce generally were kept low, while rates for manufactured goods generally were kept relatively high. The high rates for manufactured goods incentivized many manufacturers to switch to transportation by trucks. Thus, the railroads faced adverse selection. They lost many of their most profitable shippers to trucks, while still being saddled with their marginally profitable agricultural shippers. Furthermore, many of the ICC's multitude of rules and regulations stifled the introduction of such efficiencies as unit trains.

The railroads were in trouble. In the 1960s and 1970s, many went bankrupt, including, on June 21, 1970, the once venerable Penn Central, one of the largest and most important railroads in the country. Finally, even the U.S. government recognized that change was needed. In 1978, the U.S. Department of Transportation noted that "the current system of railroad regulation … is a hodgepodge of inconsistent and often anachronistic regulations that no longer correspond to the economic conditions of the railroads, the nature of intermodal competition, or the often-conflicting needs of shippers, consumers, and tax payers." ("A Short History of U.S. Freight Railroads," paper by the Policy and Economics Department of the Association of American Railroads, April 2013, page 5.)

In 1980, Harley Staggers, chair of the House Interstate and Foreign Commerce Committee, introduced an act that essentially deregulated the railroads. Under the Staggers Act, railroads could establish any rates they chose, unless the ICC determined that there was no effective competition for the service. Other provisions of the act increased the flexibility of the railroads to provide efficient service. For example, procedures for abandoning unprofitable lightly used tracks were streamlined.

The Staggers Act was a breath of fresh air. Railroads immediately started adjusting their rates to make economic sense. Unprofitable routes were dropped. With increased profits and with confidence in their future, railroads started spending more to modernize. New locomotives, freight cars, tracks, automated control systems, and computers reduced costs and increased reliability. The efficiencies allowed the railroads to reduce their rates and become more competitive with trucks and barges. According to the Association of American Railroads, the average inflation adjusted rate charged by the railroads, expressed in 2012 dollars, declined from about $0.07 per ton-mile in 1981 to below $0.03 in 2003—an amazingly large decline.

In the 1980s and 1990s, the railroad industry also enjoyed increased efficiencies through consolidating mergers. In the west, the Burlington Northern merged with the Santa Fe, and the Union Pacific merged with the Southern Pacific. As a result of the mergers, only two large railroads remained to serve the western half of the country. With increased efficiencies of scale and with reduced competition post the mergers, both the Burlington Northern Santa Fe and the Union Pacific could stabilize their earnings at a time when their rates were still declining.

During the 2001–2002 recession, Union Pacific's management reduced the railroad's costs in order to mitigate the effects of the slowdown.

Employment levels were reduced by 8.1 percent, from about 50,500 in 2000 to about 46,400 in 2003. The reduced costs permitted the railroad to enjoy larger earnings in 2003 than in 2000. However, the reductions left the Union Pacific with insufficient capacity when demand for rail transportation accelerated in 2004. The insufficient capacity led to serious congestion on many routes. An analogy might be traffic jams on a highway during rush hour. Too much traffic on a highway, and the traffic slows and backs-up. Union Pacific's congestion caused its profits to decline. Its trains took longer to reach their destinations. A railroad's revenues are a function of ton-miles, but many of its costs, especially hourly labor, are a function of time. The more the delays, the higher the costs. Furthermore, Union Pacific needed to spend large sums to hire and train an abnormally large number of new employees—and also large sums to repair and maintain old locomotives that were brought out of retirement to meet the increased demand.

Investors became aware of the earnings shortfall during the first half of 2004. On the last trading day of 2003, the price of Union Pacific's shares closed at $17.37.[1] On June 30, 2004, the shares closed at $14.86, down 14.5 percent during the six-month period. During the same period, Burlington Northern Santa Fe's shares appreciated by 8.4 percent.

It seemed logical to us that Union Pacific's congestion problems could be and would be solved within a few years. New employees could be hired and trained, new locomotives could be purchased, some trains could be rerouted away from congested lines, and new track could be added in some of the more congested corridors. Decongestion should not be a difficult task. It also seemed logical that the stronger market for rail traffic would lead to at least modest rate increases. We constructed an earnings model for Union Pacific for the year 2006 that assumed that the railroad had solved most of its problems and had increased its rates modestly. Based on these assumptions, our model projected that Union Pacific would earn close to $1.55 per share in 2006. By comparison, we expected the railroad's 2004 earnings to be only about $0.70 per share. I decided to value Union Pacific's shares conservatively at 14 times earnings. Therefore, I estimated that the shares would be worth just over $22 in 2006. In addition, the company was paying a $0.30 annual dividend. Including the dividends, I concluded that the shares, which were selling at about $14½ at the time, could provide a 55 percent total return over the two-year period 2004 to 2006. I decided to purchase the shares. They did not appear to be a particularly exciting investment opportunity, but the stock market and our stocks had been strong in 2003, and we did not have alternatives that appeared to be more attractive. Furthermore, and importantly, I believed that the shares had very solid protection from material permanent loss. Their book value was $12. The company had a strong balance sheet for a railroad. And the company and Burlington Northern were a duopoly in the western half of the United States in an industry that remained vital to the country.

There was another reason to own shares of Union Pacific rather than holding cash. Over a period of many decades, the stock market, as measured by the Standard & Poor's (S&P) 500 Index, has enjoyed an average annual total return of roughly 9½ percent—and our best guess was that returns could average somewhere around 9½ percent over the next few decades.[2] When we purchase a stock, we believe that it will appreciate by far more than the stock market appreciates. However, what if we are wrong and the stock appreciates only as much as the market? Then, if the stock is typical, it should earn an average annual return of about 9½ percent over time, which is much better than holding cash.

I note that the 9½ percent long-term upward bias of the stock market is one reason that shorting stocks generally is a bad business. To do as well as a market that tends to provide a 9½ percent annual return, a shorter of stocks must find stocks that decline by at least 9½ percent per year or that underperform the market by 19 percent. There are not many investors in the world who can outperform the stock market by 19 percent per year, and thus I imagine that there are not many investors who can find stocks that will underperform the market by 19 percent. Furthermore, when an investor is long a stock, the most he can lose is his original investment— and his upside profit potential is unlimited. When an investor is short a stock, his loss potential is unlimited if the stock happens to appreciate sharply, and his profit potential is only equal to the value of his original investment. Thus, I believe that shorting stocks generally is a miserable business, except for rare investors who have extraordinary abilities to predict when individual stocks or when markets will decline sharply.

Another reason for owning high-quality stocks is that they sometimes benefit from unanticipated surprises. That is why my old boss, Arthur Ross, continually advised me to purchase high-quality stocks and "stay in the game, Ed, stay in the game" (remember, Arthur Ross usually said things twice when he wanted to make a point).

In the case of Union Pacific, we did materially benefit from an unanticipated surprise. The surprise had to do with the price of diesel fuel. At the time we established our position in Union Pacific's shares, the price of diesel fuel was a hair over $1.50 per gallon. For the next several years, diesel prices increased steadily and sharply, reaching a high of about $4.70 per gallon in 2008. Railroads typically are three to four times more fuel efficient than trucks. Thus, to offset the higher fuel costs, trucking companies needed to increase their rates much more sharply than the railroads needed to. The sharply higher rates charged by trucking companies incentivized some shippers to switch from truck to rail. The increased demand for rail affected Union Pacific in two ways: (1) with demand exceeding supply and with trucks less competitive, Union Pacific could materially increase its rates in excess of the amounts needed to offset the increased cost of fuel; and (2) the increase in traffic delayed the solution to the congestion problem because it increased the amount of capacity that Union Pacific needed to add.

After purchasing our holding in Union Pacific, we constantly monitored the railroad's progress. From the onset, it appeared that the company was receiving larger rate increases than we had projected, but that the congestion problems were stickier than we had expected. When looking ahead, we believed that the large rate increases likely would continue and, sooner or later, the company would benefit from decongestion, and when that happened the company's earnings and share price should be buoyant.

We were increasingly excited about our investment—so excited that we also purchased shares of other railroads that also should benefit from the anticipated large increases in rates.

Wall Street generally did not agree with our excitement. On July 13, 2005, at a time when Union Pacific's shares were trading at about $16, an analyst with J. P. Morgan downgraded the shares and recommended that they be underweighted—which, in the language of Wall Street, means that they should be sold. I was intrigued that, in spite of the bearish recommendation, the analyst wrote favorable comments about the company's longer-term potential. He wrote about Union Pacific's excellent route structure and advantageous access to customers. He added that these strengths should lead to solid margin, earnings, and cash flow performance. However, the analyst was concerned that current capacity constraints and resulting operating inefficiencies would lead to short-term problems and continued disappointments that likely would take longer than a few more quarters to correct. Simply, the analyst could not wait much longer than a "few quarters" for the operational turnaround. We could.

By mid-2007, it appeared that Union Pacific was beginning to materially benefit from decongestion. In the quarter that ended on June 30, the company's average train speed was 21.6 miles per hour, up from 21.2 miles per hour during the comparable year-earlier quarter. Average dwell time (the average time a rail car spends in a terminal) was 24.7 hours in the June 2007 quarter, a large improvement from the 27.6 hours during the June 2006 quarter. The company's earnings in the first half of 2007 were up 19 percent year-over-year, in spite of adverse flash floods in several states that caused track washouts and bridge outages. Earnings estimates for the full year 2007 had increased to close to $1.50 per share—a sharp improvement versus the depressed $0.77 per share earned in 2004. Wall Street analysts had become more positive about the company's outlook, and the price of the shares had increased to above $30.

I was amused that the same J. P. Morgan analyst who in mid-2005 recommended that the shares be underweighted at $16 now was recommending that the shares be purchased at $31½. In a report dated July 17, 2006, the analyst wrote that Union Pacific's positive story was firmly intact, that the company had more pricing power than most other railroads, and that it had additional opportunities to improve its efficiencies. Ironically, the inefficiencies that were a reason not to purchase the shares in mid-2005 were a reason to purchase the shares in mid-2007. The analyst concluded that he saw meaningful upside potential for the shares.

I meet regularly with my associates at Greenhaven to discuss our ideas and holdings. By mid-2007, it was becoming clear to us that most other investors also believed that Union Pacific was benefiting from sizable rate increases and from operational efficiencies. Therefore, we concluded that a large percentage of Union Pacific's potential likely was being discounted into the price of the shares. Thus, at one of our regular meetings, we decided to start gradually selling our holding. By the end of 2007, we had sold most of our shares at an average price of roughly $31. We had held the shares for an average of about 3.7 years. During that period, the shares had slightly more than doubled, and we had earned $1.05 per share in dividends. Our average annualized return was close to 24 percent, including the dividends we had received.

The J. P. Morgan analyst who recommended underweighting Union Pacific's shares at $16 was wrong. After the recommendation, the price of the shares increased quite steadily through September 2008. My experience is that the recommendations of Wall Street analysts are wrong more often than they are correct. An investor told me that he once had an account with one of Wall Street's most respected firms. He told the Wall Street firm immediately to purchase any stock that was added to the firm's overweight list—and immediately to sell the stock when it was removed from the list. After several years of following this approach, the investor closed his account with the most respected firm because his results were particularly poor.

Why do analysts tend to be substandard stock pickers? Most analysts follow only one or a few industries and tend to have deep knowledge about the companies they follow. However, there is a large difference between knowledge and judgment. It is said that knowledge is knowing that a tomato is a fruit, but judgment is not putting it in your fruit salad. To have good judgment, you need to have the knowledge, but, in my opinion, you also need many other qualities, including common sense, stable emotions, confidence, and, quite possibly, an indefinable sixth sense.

Furthermore, in my opinion, most individuals, including securities analysts, feel more comfortable projecting current fundamentals into the future than projecting changes that will occur in the future. Current fundamentals are based on known information. Future fundamentals are based on unknowns. Predicting the future from unknowns requires the efforts of thinking, assigning probabilities, and sticking ones neck out—all efforts that human beings too often prefer to avoid.

Also, I believe it is difficult for securities analysts to embrace companies and industries that currently are suffering from poor results and impaired reputations. Often, securities analysts want to see tangible proof of better results before recommending a stock. My philosophy is that life is not about waiting for a storm to pass. It is about dancing in the rain. One usually can read a weather map and reasonably project when a storm will pass. If one waits for the moment when the sun breaks out, there is a high probability others already will have reacted to the improved prospects and already will have driven up the price of the stock—and thus the opportunity to earn large profits will have been missed.

In my opinion, one of the best articles about not waiting for storms to pass was written by Warren Buffett in a *New York Times* op-ed piece on October 17, 2008, at the height of the financial crisis. Warren Buffett wrote:

> *A simple rule dictates my buying: Be fearful when others are greedy, and be greedy when others are fearful. And most certainly, fear is now widespread, gripping even seasoned investors. To be sure, investors are right to be wary of highly leveraged entities or businesses in weak competitive positions. But fears regarding the long-term prosperity of the nation's many sound companies make no sense. These businesses will indeed suffer earnings hiccups, as*

they always have. But most major companies will be setting new profit records 5, 10, and 20 years from now. Let me be clear on one point: I can't predict the short-term movements of the stock market. I haven't the faintest idea as to whether stocks will be higher or lower a month—or a year—from now. What is likely, however, is that the market will move higher, perhaps substantially so, well before either sentiment or the economy turns up. So if you wait for the robins, spring will be over.

NOTES

1. All per-share data have been adjusted to reflect subsequent stock splits.
2. Over the 50-year period 1960–2010, the earnings underlying the S&P 500 Index grew at about a 6.8 percent average annual rate, and the average dividend yield on the Index was close to 3 percent. Looking ahead, over the longer term, we would guess that the U.S. economy could grow at about a 6 percent or so rate (half from real growth and half from inflation) and that acquisitions and share repurchases could bring corporate earnings per share growth close to 7 percent. Adding dividends, we would not be surprised if total returns remained in the range of 9 to 10 percent.

8

AMERICAN INTERNATIONAL GROUP (AIG)

Warren Buffett said: "I've never gone to bed with an ugly woman, but I've sure woke up with a few."[1] Such was our case with AIG.

The 1998–2000 bubble in technology stocks likely was a key indirect reason we purchased AIG's shares. In 2000, the bubble burst and the stock market started to decline sharply. The Nasdaq Composite Index, which is laden with technology stocks, declined from a high of 5,048 on March 10, 2000, to a low of 1,114 on October 9, 2002—a decline of 78 percent. The Standard & Poor's (S&P) 500 Index, which is more representative of the entire U.S. stock market, declined from a high of 1,521 on September 1, 2000, to a low of 801 on March 11, 2003. The magnitude of the collapse encouraged many investment committees and individual investors to seek investments that were less volatile than the stock market, and many committees and investors opted to invest in hedge funds that promised to short stocks and thus to sharply reduce downside volatility. According to BarclayHedge, the assets under the management of hedge funds increased from roughly $300 billion at the end of 2000 to more than $2 trillion by 2007.

Hedge funds typically charge their clients fees equal to 1 to 2 percent of the assets under management plus incentive fees of 20 percent of any profits. In my opinion, given this very high fee structure, hedge funds are bent to making obscure investments as opposed to, for example, purchasing blue-chip stocks. It would be difficult for a hedge fund to justify its high fees if it heavily owned shares in Exxon, 3M, Berkshire Hathaway, General Electric, Procter & Gamble, or other heavily followed and commonly owned companies. By 2006, because hedge funds had become a large force in the stock market and because hedge funds generally had shied away from blue-chip stocks, the shares of many of the largest and highest-quality companies were selling at relatively depressed prices.

In the meantime, during the period 2003 to 2005, Greenhaven's portfolios had benefited from the resurgence of the "old economy stocks" and had been abnormally buoyant. Between January 1, 2003, and December 31, 2005, a typical Greenhaven account appreciated by about 140 percent (including dividends received). By early 2006, many of our holdings had become relatively fully valued, and we sought to replace these holdings with stocks that were undervalued and out of favor. Blue-chip stocks seemed to fit the bill, and over a period of several quarters we purchased shares in GE, FedEx, 3M, and, unfortunately, AIG.

AIG's predecessor company was founded in Shanghai in 1919 by Cornelius Vander Starr, who previously had owned an ice cream store. For a number of years, the company's main business was selling life insurance policies in China. In 1926, Starr opened an office in New York City to offer casualty insurance to American companies conducting business abroad. After World War II, the communist government prohibited Starr's companies from doing business in China, but Starr more than compensated for the lost Chinese business by aggressively expanding elsewhere. After Starr died in 1967, Maurice "Hank" Greenberg became CEO of the several disparate insurance companies founded by Starr. Two of Greenberg's early actions were to merge the several companies into a newly formed AIG, and then to take the new company public.

Over the years, Hank Greenberg built AIG into a very large, highly profitable, and highly regarded "growth" company. During the 15-year period 1989 to 2004, AIG's revenues and earnings both grew at a 14.1 percent compound annual growth rate (CAGR), and the company's share price increased at about a 17 percent CAGR. AIG was a winner.

However, in 2004 and 2005, the company hit legal bumps when it was accused of several wrongdoings, including engaging in sham reinsurance transactions that were designed to bolster its reserves. Hank Greenberg was forced to resign in early 2005, and Martin Sullivan became the new CEO. Whereas the S&P 500 Index appreciated moderately between 2004 and 2006, AIG's shares remained flattish. In the spring of 2006, I reasoned that the 2004 and 2005 scandals had adversely affected the price of AIG's shares, that the shares were out of favor with hedge funds and other aggressive investors, and that, for these reasons, we now had the opportunity to purchase the shares at a materially undervalued price.

I started analyzing AIG by reading the company's Form 10-K and annual report. There was nothing in the 10-K that surprised me. When reading the annual report, I realized that the reported earnings and balance sheets of any insurance company are no more than estimates because managements, actuarial firms, and independent accountants must estimate the magnitude of recent and future losses—and such estimates often are no more than educated guesses. However, AIG had taken a $1.82 billion pretax charge in late 2005 to increase its reserves, and my reasoning was that the new management had every incentive to take as large a charge as possible. After all, the new management could blame the old management for the charge, and a large charge now would lead to larger earnings in the future. Thus, the charge gave me some comfort that AIG's reserves now were accurately stated, if not conservatively stated.

Insurance companies need to be financially strong, and in the annual report's letter to shareholders, management emphasized that "AIG remains among the most strongly capitalized organizations in our industry." AIG's credit ratings were the equivalent of AA, and management commented that "at these levels, AIG's ratings are among the highest of any insurance and financial services organization in the world."

I telephoned two friends who were CEOs of insurance companies. CEOs often do not like to praise their competitors, but both my friends gave AIG rave reviews. In particular, both stated that AIG's size and capital strength gave the company a competitive advantage. Medium-sized insurance companies often do not have sufficient capital and scope to meet the insurance needs of large, international Fortune 500 companies. Therefore, AIG sometimes faced limited competition on very large policies—and limited competition often led to high premiums and high profits.

One of my CEO friends invited my wife and me to have dinner at his home with Martin Sullivan, AIG's new CEO. I leapt at the opportunity. Of course, one cannot judge the capabilities of a CEO from a three-hour social evening, but nonetheless, I found Martin Sullivan to be affable, knowledgeable, and highly intelligent. I left the dinner with a positive feeling about AIG's leadership.

After additional reading, thinking, and debating, I made a model of AIG's possible future earnings per share (EPS) in a normal environment. I used "normalized" earnings because the reported earnings of an insurance company can vary from year to year, especially due to the occurrences of hurricanes or other catastrophes. My conclusion was that the company's normalized 2008 EPS should be about $7 per share. The $7 would equal about a 15 percent return on a projected 2008 book value of about $46.50 per share. The company seemed to earn a 15 percent return on book value in normal years, so the $7 EPS estimate appeared to be reasonable.

Next, I valued AIG. Upon reflection, my best thinking was that AIG's shares were worth close to an average price-to-earnings (PE) ratio, or about 15 times earnings. Therefore, I concluded that, in 2008, AIG's shares would be worth roughly $105, or nearly twice their existing price of about $55. Based on these numbers and the first-class reputation of the company, I started building a position in the shares.

The year 2006 ended up to be good for AIG. EPS, before some unusual accounting adjustments for hedging, was a favorable $5.88. In the fourth quarter of the year, management studied the company's capital position and concluded that the company was overcapitalized by $15 to $20 billion. As a result of the study, in March 2007, management authorized the repurchase of $8 billion shares of the company's stock, and in May, management increased the company's dividend by 20 percent. I was smiling.

Toward the end of 2007, there was some general nervousness in the financial markets, and the price of AIG's shares slipped from about $57 at the end of September to about $49 at the end of December. The shares continued to slip some in early 2008 and then declined sharply to a low of $33 when it appeared that Bear Stearns might declare bankruptcy. But the shares started to recover after J. P. Morgan announced that it would purchase Bear Stearns, and by mid-April the shares had recovered to the $40 level.

In late April, the price of AIG's shares still was materially below our cost basis. From time to time, one or more of Greenhaven's holdings run into headwinds. The economy and the financial markets are cyclical. Headwinds come with the territory of investing. When shares of one of our holdings are weak, we usually revisit the company's longer-term fundamentals. If the longer-term fundamentals have not changed, we normally will continue to hold the shares, if not purchase more. In the case of AIG, it appeared to us that the longer-term fundamentals remained intact. The company did have to report losses from the marking to market of a number of assets, including derivative contracts in its Financial Products subsidiary, which insured such financial risks as bank loans. The markdowns largely were necessitated by generally increasing yields on higher-risk assets, not by concerns that AIG's loss experiences materially would deteriorate. Therefore, our reasoning was that, when the derivative contracts matured, most or all of the losses would be reversed. In Berkshire Hathaway's 2007 annual report, Warren Buffett had complained about the need to mark derivative contracts to market: "Changes in the value of a derivative contract … must be applied each quarter to earnings. Thus, our derivative positions will sometimes cause large swings in reported earnings, even though Charlie (Munger) and I might believe the intrinsic value of these positions has changed little. He and I will not be bothered by these swings. … And we hope you won't either." Further, we reasoned that, if the credit rating companies or the regulators were concerned about the write-downs, AIG could always raise cash and capital by selling new common shares, preferred shares, or subordinated debt. Indeed, on May 8, AIG announced that it would raise about $20 billion of new capital through the sale of new common shares and subordinated debentures.

However, the nervousness continued, and during June and July 2008, AIG's shares generally sold between $20 and $25. In mid-August, I noticed that a key director of AIG, who at the time chaired the board's finance committee and who had previously chaired the audit committee, had purchased 30,000 AIG's shares for his own account on August 12. These purchases gave me considerable comfort. Certainly, the chair of the finance committee would not purchase shares if he were concerned about AIG's future, and certainly he should be unusually well informed about the fundamentals of the company.

On the morning of September 15, all hell broke loose when Lehman filed for Chapter 11 bankruptcy protection. Katie bar the door. The filing triggered a meltdown that fed on itself. Extreme illiquidity in the financial markets caused asset values to fall sharply. The decline in asset values caused financial institutions to mark down the carrying value of their assets, which, in turn, caused sharp reductions in their credit ratings. Sharp reductions in credit ratings required financial institutions to raise capital and, in the case of AIG, to post collateral on its derivative contracts. But the near freezing of the financial markets prevented the requisite raising of capital and cash and thus caused a further deterioration in creditworthiness, which further increased the need for new capital and cash, and so on. In the wake of the collapse of Lehman and the near freezing of the financial markets, the price of AIG's shares fell sharply. The company needed a large influx of cash to post as collateral, but with the markets close to frozen, the cash could not be raised. On Tuesday night, September 16, the

U.S. government agreed to provide the requisite cash in return for a lion's share of the ownership of AIG. As soon as I read the agreement, it was clear to me that we had a large permanent loss in our holdings in AIG.

The failing of Lehman and the resulting severe financial crisis were outlier events that had not been part of our thinking or planning. Over the next few weeks, I worked long hours trying to get a handle on what was happening. It was difficult to think clearly and unemotionally in the midst of the most serious economic crisis since the Great Depression. Given the dangers and uncertainties, we had to act. Within several weeks of the failure of Lehman, we sold the bulk of our holdings in financial service companies and we sold several stocks that had not declined sharply and, therefore, that had become less attractive relative to the stock market in general. These actions increased our cash holdings to about 40 percent of the value of our portfolios.

During the next few months, we thought long and hard about the economic environment and about our portfolios. It soon became clear to me that our nation faced two interrelated, yet disparate, problems: (1) the financial crisis and (2) a deep recession. I decided that, as long as the financial crisis continued, we would hold on to our large holdings of cash. I was fearful that, if the crisis did not end, the deep recession could turn into another Great Depression. However, I reasoned that if the crisis ended, the opportunity to reinvest the cash in abnormally undervalued common stocks likely would be compelling. In my opinion, many corporations had sharply reduced their inventory levels during the financial crisis in order to raise cash, and these inventory reductions were a major cause of the recession. Once the crisis ended, corporations likely would replenish at least some of their inventories—and the replenishment would be a stimulant to the overall economy. Furthermore, during the crisis many individuals and corporations deferred purchasing large-ticket items that they had either needed or wanted. I believed that after the crisis ended, there would be at least some deferred demand for many goods and services. Also, by late 2008, it was clear to me that the U.S. government and the Federal Reserve Bank would take aggressive actions to stimulate the economy. Thus, I concluded that, once the financial crisis ended, there would be a high probability that the economy would bounce back some, maybe sharply.

In late 2008 and early 2009, we carefully monitored the interest rate spreads between U.S. treasuries and lesser quality debt instruments—and we also searched for other signs that the financial crisis was continuing or was abating. By March, interest rate spreads had narrowed and substantial confidence had returned to the financial system, and I decided to reinvest the cash in our portfolios. Between the end of 2007 and March 31, 2009, while the S&P 500 Index had declined by about 45 percent, the subsector of the Index that was composed of industrial companies had declined by about 54 percent. Industrial companies are more economically sensitive than most other types of companies (such as consumer durables, pharmaceuticals, and utilities), so it is not surprising that industrial stocks declined by more than the market as a whole. When purchasing stocks in the spring of 2009, we mainly purchased shares of industrial companies. They not only were more depressed than most other sectors of the market, but also they would more directly benefit from a bounce-back of the economy. Our strategy succeeded. A typical Greenhaven portfolio, after losing about 38 percent of its value in the disastrous year 2008, appreciated by roughly 47 percent in 2009 and 21 percent in 2010. By the end of 2010, the value of a typical Greenhaven portfolio was close to 10 percent higher than at the end of 2007.

AIG had been a disaster for Greenhaven but not for the U.S. government. After the crisis, AIG skinnied down and enjoyed good operating earnings. The U.S. government benefited from the recovery in AIG's fortunes and gradually reduced its investment in the company, selling the last of its holdings on December 11, 2012. According to the U.S. Treasury, the Federal Reserve Bank and the U.S. Treasury together earned a $22.7 billion profit on its "investment" in AIG.

Some criticize the U.S. government for bailing out financial institutions during the financial crisis. I disagree with the critics. As one of the only suppliers of capital to financial institutions during the crisis, the government had the bargaining power of a monopoly and therefore was in a position to negotiate particularly favorable terms. Most of the financial institutions, including AIG, continued to have strong and viable businesses. Their problem was liquidity, not solvency. No wonder the government made a profit on most of its bailouts.

Furthermore, and most importantly, the bailouts helped restore confidence in the financial system—and the restored confidence helped the economy climb from recessionary levels. The bailouts were a pragmatic partial solution to a very serious problem. Many idealists took the position that, in principle, the government never should bail out private enterprises. I believe that humans and institutions need to be pragmatic and flexible and that strong ideologies and tunnel visions can lead to failures that end up hurting people.

A few weeks after the collapse of AIG's shares, a friend and client asked me if I had learned anything from the horribly failed investment. I told him that we were still in the fog of war and that I would have a clearer picture of our mistake after the financial crisis ended. Months later, I did reflect on the investment. I reviewed the work we had performed and the information we had learned, both of which were extensive. I then asked myself the question: if I had to make the purchase decision today based on what we knew then, would I still make the same decision to purchase the shares? My answer was "yes"—and my conclusion was that, in the investment business, relatively unpredictable outlier developments sometimes can quickly derail otherwise attractive investments. It comes with the territory. So while we work hard to reduce the risks of large permanent loss, we cannot completely eliminate large risks. However, we can draw a line on how much risk we are willing to accept—a line that provides sufficient apparent protection and yet prevents us from being so risk averse that we turn down too many attractive opportunities. One should not invest with the precept that the next 100-year storm is around the corner.

Luckily, in practice, usually we become aware of adverse changes sufficiently early that we can sell shares before any loss becomes too large. For example, in 2014, we purchased shares in Praxair, a manufacturer of oxygen, nitrogen, hydrogen, and other industrial gases. The shares appeared undervalued, and we believed that the company's earnings growth likely would accelerate because an aggressive new management at Air Products, a key competitor, would attempt to control capacity and increase prices. A few quarters after we purchased the shares, it became apparent to us that the new management at Air Products was more interested in reducing costs than in increasing prices. Furthermore, about 14 percent of Praxair's earnings came from Brazil, where the value of the real (Brazil's currency) suddenly had declined sharply because of economic and political problems. We were fearful that the decline would be long lasting. Thus, our original projections and valuations for Praxair had become too optimistic. We reacted by selling the shares at a modest loss.

In my investment career, I frequently have sold shares at modest losses after realizing that my original valuations were too high. We have suffered many Praxairs. I find that investing is not about earning a favorable return on every holding—it is about developing a favorable batting average.

NOTES

1. Warren Buffett, Berkshire Hathaway Inc. 2007 annual report, p. 9.

9

LOWE'S

Lowe's is the second-largest home improvement retailer. Through about 1,850 stores spread throughout the United States and Canada, Lowe's sells roughly 40,000 house-related items, including lumber, wallboard, flooring, appliances, kitchen and bathroom cabinets, plumbing fixtures, lighting fixtures, paint, power tools, outdoor furniture, grass seed, plants, and fertilizer. The company's sales volumes closely track with the strength of the housing industry.

Lowe's was founded in 1921 when Lucius S. Lowe opened a hardware store in North Wilkesboro, North Carolina. After Lucius Lowe died in 1940, the store was owned and operated by several family members, and especially by Carl Buchan, a son-in-law. In the 1950s, Buchan opened several new stores that sold building supplies as well as hardware. Buchan died suddenly in 1960. Robert Strickland, the new CEO, took the company public in 1961 and continued to expand its footprint. Lowe's revenues increased from $25 million in 1960, to more than $150 million in 1970, and to nearly $900 million in 1980.

Historically, Lowe's had concentrated on selling to the professional builder. But when the market for new houses weakened in 1980, the company started redesigning its stores to appeal to the do-it-yourself homeowner. At about that time, a new competitor, The Home Depot, started opening big-box warehouse stores that typically were five times larger than the stores operated by Lowe's. By 1989, it was clear that Home Depot's large store format was the way of the future. Lowe's took an impairment charge in 1991 to close smaller stores—and management then started aggressively opening big-box stores to compete with Home Depot. In 1993 alone, Lowe's nearly doubled its floor space by opening 57 new stores, each averaging close to 100,000 square feet in size. The race with Home Depot was on.

In 1993,[1] Lowe's had revenues of $4.54 billion and Home Depot had revenues of $9.24 billion. Over the next 10 years, Lowe's revenues increased at a 21 percent average annual rate to $30.84 billion and Home Depot's revenues increased at a similar rate. Both companies grew rapidly at the expense of small building supply and hardware stores. Small stores simply could not compete with the purchasing powers, distribution efficiencies, merchandise varieties, efficiencies of scale, and low real estate costs enjoyed by the two big-box retailers.

Lowe's prospered during the 2001–2005 period. The company not only benefited from the boom in housing, but also from taking market share from Home Depot, which was suffering from some self-inflicted merchandising problems. During the five-year period that ended on January 31, 2006, Lowe's sales per store (comps) increased at a 5.4 percent average annual rate, while Home Depot's comps only increased at a 2.5 percent average rate. Lowe's was flying high. The company's earnings climbed from $0.53 per share in 2000 to $1.73 per share in 2005. And the price of its shares increased 150 percent during the five-year period, hitting $34.85 in late 2005. Lowe's shareholders were smiling.

Then, the housing boom turned into a bust. In the three-year period 2007 to 2009, Lowe's comps declined by an aggregate of 17.8 percent—a near disaster. Earnings, leveraged downward by the weak sales, fell by 39 percent, from $1.99 per share in 2006 to $1.21 in 2009, and earnings would have declined further if management had not taken strong steps to reduce costs. The price of the company's shares fell to a low of $13 in March 2009.

The housing bust was worse than I had imagined. Overbuilding during the years 2004 to 2006 and a high level of foreclosures led to a glut of empty homes. With vacant homes at record levels, the construction of new housing units collapsed from close to 2 million in 2006 to only 585,000 in 2011.

In the spring of 2011, the prevailing opinion on Wall Street was that the housing market would continue to be very weak for some time, largely because of a "shadow inventory" of homes near foreclosure that likely would materially add to the inventory of unsold homes. Because of this prevailing negative sentiment, the shares of housing-related companies were selling at depressed prices. I was intrigued by the depressed prices and by the logic that the housing industry eventually had to recover strongly. Therefore, I decided to conduct my own study of the market. My conclusion was that the market could turn surprisingly strong within the next several years. My logic and methodology were as follows.

First, I estimated how many new housing units were required each year to satisfy normal demand. Normal demand is equal to the net increase in the number of families in the United States, plus the number of houses torn down each year, plus the increase in the number of vacation and other second homes.

In 2011, there were about 131 million housing units in the United States. Between 2000 and 2010 the population of the United States increased at a 0.92 percent compound annual growth rate (CAGR) from 282.16 million to 309.33 million. I reasoned that if the population continued to increase at a 0.92 percent CAGR, there would be a need for about 1,200,000 additional housing units per year (131 million times 0.92 percent). I also read a lengthy report issued in September 2010 by Harvard University's Joint Center for Housing Studies that predicted that net family formations during the decade 2010 to 2020 would be in the range of 1,180,000 to 1,280,000 per year. After reading a few other studies, I decided to estimate that at least 1,200,000 new housing units would be required in a normal year to meet the annual net increase in family forma-tions plus the increase in demand for second homes. I also estimated that about 300,000 additional new housing units would be required annually to replace houses that were demolished because of age, fire, flood, location, and so on. Therefore, I concluded that at least 1,500,000 new housing units were needed in a normal year.

Before conducting further analysis, I decided to check my 1,500,000 estimate against historical data. In the 20-year period 1980 to 1999, the average annual number of housing units completed in the United States was 1,430,000. The population of the United States during the 20-year period averaged about 250 million. Adjusted to the 2011 population of 311 million, 1,430,000 completions would be the equivalent of about 1,780,000 units in 2011. Looking at a more recent period, annual hous-ing completions during four years, 2000 through 2003, averaged about 1,620,000, in spite of the adverse effects of 9/11 and the mild recession. These data gave me confidence that, even if demographics were somewhat less favorable post the financial crisis, my 1,500,000 estimate for normal demand was reasonable, if not conservative.

The number of new housing units built in 2010 in the United States was only 650,000, and it appeared that the number would decline to below 600,000 in 2011, or at a depression level of only 40 percent of estimated normal demand. Construction could not remain at 40 percent of normal demand forever. People have to live somewhere. It was clear to me that the housing market would recover and that the recovery would be very strong, with housing completions eventually increasing 2.5-fold to about the 1,500,000 level. The remaining unknown was the timing of the recovery.

To estimate the possible timing of the recovery, I used Census Bureau data on housing completions to calculate that, if the normal annual demand for new housing is 1,500,000 units, then 1,400,000 excess houses were built during the boom years 2004 through 2007. Another consider-ation was the effect of foreclosures on the housing market, a consideration that seemed to befuddle many Wall Street analysts. When thinking about foreclosures, I adopted the following approach. When a house is foreclosed, the foreclosure adds to the inventory overhang only if the former occupant moves in with another family (typically a parent or a friend), as opposed to purchasing another house or leasing a rental unit. Thus, if I were able to estimate the increase in "doubled-up" households, I would know the number of house vacancies that were created by the foreclosures or by the loss of jobs. Such figures were available. The number of doubled-up families had increased by about 2 million during the years 2008 through 2010 and seemed to have stabilized at that level.

Therefore, before consideration of the recent underbuilding of housing units, I concluded that the overbuilding in the 2004–2007 period and the foreclosures in the 2008–2010 period increased the inventory of vacant homes by about 3,400,000 housing units (1,400,000 from overbuilding during 2004–2007 plus the 2 million vacated because of foreclosures). Again using Census Bureau data, I then calculated that the underbuilding during the years 2008 through 2010 totaled 1,900,000 units (vs. the normal annual need of 1,500,000 new units) and therefore that, during the entire 2003–2010 period, the inventory of vacant homes increased by 1,500,000 units. Since housing inventories at the end of 2003 seemed to be at normal levels, I concluded that the estimated inventory overhang at the end of 2010 was approximately 1,500,000 units. In 2011, only about 600,000 new housing units were being built. If construction continued at the 600,000 level and if normal demand was 1,500,000, the housing industry would be in balance by late 2012, assuming that the number of doubled-up families had stabilized, which seemed to be the case.

I was excited that we had a concept about a probable strong upturn in the housing market that was not shared by most others. I believed that the existing negativism about housing was due to the proclivity of human beings to uncritically project recent trends into the future and to overly dwell on existing problems. When analyzing companies and industries, I tend to be an optimist by nature and a pragmatist through effort. In terms of the proverbial glass of water, it is never half empty, but always half full— and, as a pragmatist, it is twice as large as it needs to be.

After I became enthusiastic about an upturn in the housing market, I started looking for investments that would benefit from the improvement. My first instinct was to study the publicly owned homebuilders. However, their balance sheets were not strong, and I was concerned about risks of insolvency if the housing market did not improve over the next few years. I continually attempt to minimize risks of permanent loss and continually am mindful of Warren Buffett's two rules for successful inventing: "Rule number one is never lose money; rule number two is never forget rule number one."

My second instinct was to study the home improvement retailers, and I soon became excited about Lowe's, largely because I believed that the company would benefit from two positive changes: (1) the upturn in the housing market and (2) improved merchandising. During the years 2001 to 2005, when Home Depot was suffering from merchandising problems and when Lowe's was gaining market share, Lowe's apparently became complacent and let its merchandising slip. The company now needed to study each product it sold and eliminate poorly selling products, introduce new exciting products, obtain lower prices from its suppliers, optimize the prices it charged its customers, find the optimum selling space for each product, adjust inventory levels to minimize stock-outs and the need for markdowns, and modernize advertising and signage. Lowe's management seemed serious about improving the company's merchandising. I reasoned that the improvements required attention and effort, not rocket science, and that there was a high probability that substantial progress could be made within two to three years.

After studying Lowe's financials and other fundamentals, I constructed a model of normalized 2014 earnings. My model assumed that the housing industry recovered and that the company's merchandising materially improved. First, I estimated what revenues might be in 2014. In 2011, Lowe's stores contained a total of 197 million square feet of selling space. The company was projecting that its selling space would increase at a 1 percent annual rate. Consequently, I projected that its selling space in 2014 would total 203 million square feet. The company's sales per square foot in 2010 were $250, down from $302 in 2003. I believed that the company's revenues in 2003 were at a normal level. Therefore, I assumed that sales per square foot would return to the $302 level, before adjusting for subsequent inflation, and to $337 assuming that the inflation rate between 2003 and 2014 averaged 1 percent.[2] Thus, I projected that Lowe's normalized revenues in 2014 could be $337 per square foot times 203 million square feet, or $68.4 billion.

Next, I projected operating profit margins. The company's margins in 2003 were 10.5 percent before nonrecurring costs to open new stores. I saw no reason why the company's margins could not return to the 10.5 percent level by 2014 if the housing industry recovered and if the company's merchandizing improved sufficiently.

Operating margins of 10.5 percent on $68.4 billion of sales would produce $7,180 million of operating profit. To calculate after-tax earnings, I subtracted projected interest expense of $275 million and taxes at a 38 percent rate. To then calculate earnings per share (EPS), I divided projected after-tax earnings by the 1.4 billion shares that were outstanding. My conclusion was that normal EPS in 2014 could be a bit over $3.

Finally, I valued the shares. There was a lot to like about Lowe's. It had a strong balance sheet. It was generating large amounts of excess cash. It essentially was a duopoly. It enjoyed a favorable reputation. However, Home Depot and Lowe's had saturated the United States with stores, and therefore, once housing recovered, Lowe's future growth likely would be relatively slow. On balance, I decided to value Lowe's at 16 times earnings, which is slightly above the average historical price-to-earnings (PE) ratio of the stock market. Therefore, I believed that Lowe's shares in 2014 would be worth slightly in excess of $48. The shares at the time were trading at about $24. They appeared to be a bargain. I started purchasing the shares and over the next several months built a large holding.

On December 7, 2011, Lowe's management held a meeting for analysts and shareholders. At the meeting, the company disclosed its "road map" projections for 2015. Importantly, the projections assumed that housing prices only increased modestly by 2015 and that housing completions only reached the 900,000 to 1 million level. The company's road map estimated that revenues would increase at a 4.5 percent average annual rate to $58.7 billion in 2015 and that operating profit margins would increase to 10 percent.

The road map also projected that Lowe's would repurchase $18 billion of its shares over the four year period 2012 to 2015. The $18 billion was a mind-boggling surprise. The entire market value of the company at the time was only $35 billion, so the company was planning to repurchase 51 percent of its existing market value over the next four years. The company projected that the repurchases would reduce the number of shares outstanding from about 1,400 million to 900 million. The extremely aggressive repurchase program would materially increase Lowe's earnings per share. It also was a strong signal of management's confidence in the company's future as well as its interest in the price of Lowe's shares.

How could the company afford to repurchase $18 billion of its shares? There were several considerations. Earnings would increase sharply. Capital expenditures would trail depreciation by an aggregate of $1 billion because the company did not intend to open many new stores. New computer systems and the new merchandizing programs would reduce the company's investment in inventories by $1 billion. Also, the company would generate close to $7 billion of cash by increasing its debt. Management believed that the company's balance sheet was underleveraged and that the increased debt could be supported by cash flows and asset values.

After the December 7 meeting, I revised my earnings model. I revise models frequently because my initial models rarely are close to being accurate. Usually, they are no better than directional. But they usually do lead me in the right direction, and, importantly, the process of constructing a model forces me to consider and weigh the central fundamentals of a company that will determine the company's future value.

My revised model focused on projected results for the year 2015. Management was projecting 4.5 percent average annual revenues growth without a major recovery in housing. After thinking and making some submodels, I projected that average annual revenue growth could be 6.5 percent assuming that the housing recovery was quite, but not very, strong.

If the annual growth rate were 6.5 percent, revenues in 2015 would be about $64 billion.

I had a problem determining the operating profit margin I should use in the revised model. Management had stated that each $1 of incremental revenues would increase operating profits by about $0.20. Based on my knowledge of the company, the 20 percent incremental made sense. Given a 20 percent incremental, if Lowe's revenues increased for four years at 6.5 percent per year instead of the road map's 4.5 percent per year, then the company's projected operating margin in 2015 would be 1.6 percent above the road map's 10 percent (20 percent of 2 percent for four years). However, the company's margins had never been as high as 11.6 percent before, and my instincts guided me to a more conservative estimate. I settled for 10.5 percent.

Continuing with the revised model, if revenues were $64 billion, operating margins were 10.5 percent, interest expenses were $650 million (higher than my previous model's $275 million because the company planned to increase its debt by close to $7 billion), income taxes were at a 38 percent rate, and the number of shares outstanding were 920 million, EPS would be $4.10. We had paid only about $24 for the shares. If 2015 earnings were close to $4.10, the shares should be a complete winner, and if we were too optimistic and earnings were only at the $3 level, the shares still should be an attractive investment. Furthermore, because of the quality of the company and because its shares were selling at a depressed price, our risks of permanent loss were low. Lowe's was a sweet dream investment.

Over the next eight months, the price of Lowe's shares fluctuated some, but on balance remained relatively flat. In August 2012, the shares were trading at $27 to $28—not much above what we paid for them. Then, in the fall of 2012, the housing market started to improve. The seasonally adjusted annualized rate of housing starts, which had remained in the range of 700,000 to 750,000 during the first half of 2012, increased to 854,000 in September and to 983,000 in December. It appeared that the housing recovery was under way, and Lowe's shares responded, rising to $35.52 at year-end 2012 and to about $45 in August 2013.

In late September 2013, as I was walking off a tennis court in a good mood because I had played well and had handily defeated my opponent, I was approached by another money manager who asked for my current opinion of Lowe's shares. After I responded favorably, he agreed that shares still looked attractive, but then added: "But aren't you concerned that the stock market will decline sharply if the budget impasse in Congress leads to a shutdown of the government?" The other manager was clearly concerned about Washington and its effect on the economy and the stock market. He was selling shares to raise cash. I answered that I had no idea what the stock market would do in the near term. I virtually never do. I strongly believe in Warren Buffett's dictum that he never has an opinion on the stock market because, if he did, it would not be any good, and it might interfere with opinions that are good. I have monitored the short-term market predictions of many intelligent and knowledgeable investors and have found that they were correct about half the time. Thus, one would do just as well by flipping a coin.

I feel the same way about predicting the short-term direction of the economy, interest rates, commodities, or currencies. There are too many variables that need to be identified and weighed. I agree with the gist of the story about the only two economists in the world who fully understand current trends in interest rates. They both live in Switzerland. And their views are diametrically opposed to each other's.

I had a personal experience being wrong about the near-term price of two commodities: crude oil and natural gas. The price of both increased sharply between mid-2007 and early summer 2008: crude from about $75 per barrel to over $140 and natural gas from about $5 per thousand cubic feet to more than $10. A friend and I were worried that the high prices would hurt the U.S. economy and balance of payments—and transfer substantial wealth from deserving middle-income and poorer Americans to undeserving and potentially hostile OPEC countries. We decided to take action. We wrote a paper on the need for a U.S. energy policy to encourage both domestic production and energy conservation. We called several senators and congressmen whom we knew and suggested that they actively work to solve our energy problem. Our pleas fell on deaf ears. One senator told us that he agreed with everything we said and that he had written a book on the subject several years earlier. His office sent us a copy of the book. I read it. It was hogwash.

As it turned out, our concerns were overblown. We did not foresee that energy prices would plummet during the financial crisis and deep recession. And neither did we foresee that the technologies of horizontal drilling and multistage fracking would lead to large production increases of crude oil and natural gas—actually leading to a glut of gas. I was wrong about the prices of oil and gas, and if I tried to predict the short-term prices of almost any other commodity, or any currency, or any market, I likely would be wrong about as often as I would be right.

While Greenhaven spends little time studying the short-term outlook for the economy and the stock market, we do spend considerable time studying the short-term fundamentals of the companies in our portfolios, and by the fall of 2014, it had become apparent to us that Lowe's was making considerable progress improving its merchandising. On November 19, the company reported that its comps (sales per store) had increased by a surprisingly strong 5.1 percent in the quarter that ended on October 31 and that its EPS had increased year over year by 25.5 percent. Robert Niblock (chairman and CEO) attributed a large part of the progress to the "internal initiatives that we have been working on." Greenhaven was becoming excited that Lowe's seemed to be entering a period of accelerated revenues and EPS growth.

Then, on December 11, Lowe's held a half-day meeting for analysts and investors. At the meeting, management projected that, between 2014 and 2017, the company's revenues would increase at a 4.5 to 5.0 percent CAGR, that its operating margins would increase by 2.5 percent to about 11 percent, and that its EPS would increase at a 20.5 percent CAGR to $4.70. Importantly, we believed that the assumptions behind Lowe's projections were conservative, and if the U.S. economy happened to return to trend line growth, Lowe's revenues, margins, and earnings could exceed management's expectations. I reworked my earnings model and concluded that, should the U.S. economy improve to trend line, Lowe's could earn as much as $5.50 per share in 2017. Clearly, we had a winner—and the price of the shares reflected the positive earnings and outlook, appreciating to $67.50 at year-end 2014, which was 160 percent above what we had paid for the shares in 2011. We were happy campers—very happy campers.

NOTES

1. Lowe's and Home Depot's fiscal years end on January 31; when referring to a particular year, I am referring to the year that ended on the following January 31.
2. The actual inflation rate between 2003 and 2011 was about 2 percent for building materials and garden supplies, but I believed that Lowe's prices likely increased somewhat less than average.

10

WHIRLPOOL CORPORATION

Once we became excited about the probable recovery in the housing market, we decided to invest about 20 percent of the funds we managed in stocks that should benefit from the recovery. Lowe's was our number one pick. After researching a few dozen other companies, we purchased a medium-sized position in Whirlpool Corporation and small positions in The Home Depot, Lennox International (a manufacturer of air conditioners and furnaces), and Mohawk Industries (a manufacturer of carpets and other flooring materials). Why was Lowe's our number one pick and our largest position? Simply, Lowe's appeared to be materially more undervalued than Home Depot and the other larger capitalization stocks we researched. Home Depot had made a number of excellent merchandising decisions and was operating on eight cylinders. Lowe's was sputtering some, and the price of its shares reflected the sputtering. In 2011, Lowe's had revenues of $50 billion and a market value (the price of shares times the number of shares outstanding) of only about $24 billion. Therefore, an investor received about $2.08 of revenues for each $1 of market value.

Home Depot had revenues of roughly $70 billion and a market value of $56 billion. Thus, an investor received only $1.25 of revenues for each $1 of market value. The comparison of revenues to market value was one of many comparisons we performed. All the comparisons clearly showed that, if Lowe's engine revved up and purred, we could make far more money in Lowe's than in Home Depot.

Liquidity was another consideration. Lowe's had a market value of $24 billion. Lennox and Mohawk had market values of only $2 billion and $4 billion. Their shares did not trade in sufficient quantities to permit us to easily purchase or sell large quantities of the shares. Liquidity helps protect us from permanent losses. We do make mistakes, and when we make a mistake, we sometimes wish to exit the mistake quickly. We are victims of our own success. Because our strategies and disciplines have been successful over the years, we have earned high returns, and because we have earned high returns, we have materially more assets under management than if our results had been less favorable. The increased size of assets under management definitely reduces our flexibility and therefore our future returns. No good deed goes unpunished.

As it turned out, when housing-related stocks started to rebound in 2012, Home Depot, Lennox, and Mohawk initially outperformed Lowe's. Investors generally had opted for the cleaner and clearer fundamentals. Lowe's merchandising problems were an uncertainty—and many investors shy away from uncertainties. The price of Home Depot's, Lennox's, and Mohawk's shares continued to climb sharply in early 2013, and we then sold the shares for roughly twice what we paid for them.

Of our five housing-related investments, Whirlpool was my second favorite. The company's shares were selling at a depressed price because the company's earnings had been under pressure from sharply increased costs for steel and other raw materials and from weak demand for appliances. We reasoned that there was a high probability that the cost of raw materials would stabilize or decline and that the demand for appliances would increase sharply as the housing market recovered. We projected that the company could earn roughly $20 per share five years hence and that the shares could then be worth $250 to $300. The shares were trading at about $80 at the time we performed our analysis. Thus, if all went well, the shares would be a superb investment.

Whirlpool was founded in 1911 by Lou Upton as the Upton Machine Company. Until that time, clothes washing machines were wooden tubs. Housewives filled the tubs with clothes, water, and soap and then scrubbed the clothes by hand. Upton added an electric motor to the tub. Almost immediately, Upton received an order for 100 of his newfangled washing machines from a company named Federal Electric. However, a problem soon arose when a cast-iron gear broke in many of the machines. Upton quickly replaced the defective part with a new gear made from steel. The problem was solved, and Federal Electric was so impressed by Upton's speedy reaction and business ethics that it ordered an additional 100 machines. A company was born.

In 1929, Upton merged his company into the Nineteen Hundred Washer Company of New York, which evidently was an innovative company in spite of its totally uninnovative and awkward name. After producing airplane parts during World War II, the Nineteen Hundred Washer Company, anticipating a large postwar demand for home appliances, successfully introduced a broader line of appliances. In 1949, the company's management demonstrated infinite wisdom by changing the name of the company to Whirlpool. At the time of the name change, Whirlpool's revenues were $48 million. Over the next 50 years, Whirlpool continued to aggressively introduce new products and acquire other companies. By 1999, the company's revenues had reached $10,511 million, a 219-fold increase versus 1949.

I find that the following data are both interesting and important. Whirlpool's growth in revenues from $48 million in 1949 to $10,511 million in 1999 seems huge, but actually equates to a compound annual growth rate (CAGR) of only 11.4 percent. This means that if the company's profit margins and price-to-earnings (PE) ratio remained flat during the 50-year period, an investor's average annual return during the 50-year period would have been only 11.4 percent, plus dividends that were received. Since Greenhaven strives for annual returns of 15 to 20 percent, if we had owned Whirlpool for the 50-year interval, the investment would have been subpar, in spite of the 219-fold increase in revenues.

In the 1950s, the appliance industry was a growth industry, as many homeowners purchased dishwashers, freezers, and clothes dryers for the first time. During the 12-year period 1949 to 1961, Whirlpool's revenues grew from $48 million to $437 million, which is equal to a CAGR of 20.2 percent. During the next 38 years, the appliance industry matured and slowed, and Whirlpool's growth slowed to an 8.7 percent average annual rate. I believe that there is an important lesson in this. Over time, the growth rates of almost all technologies, products, and services slow because of saturation, obsolescence, or competition. Many investors tend to project high growth rates far into the future without fully considering forces that eventually will lead to slower growth. In the late 1960s and early 1970s, it became fashionable among many investors to purchase growth stocks with the intention of holding the stocks forever. These investors focused on about 50 stocks that appeared to have superior growth characteristics. Due to the popularity of the stocks, their prices rose substantially, and they sold at historically high PE ratios. The growth stock investors made the argument that the high PE ratios were neither a relevancy nor a risk, and therefore should be ignored. Their logic was that if a company was growing at a 20 percent rate and if the company's stock was going to be held for many decades, the investor would earn a high return even if the PE ratio declined materially over the decades. For example, if shares of a company growing at a 20 percent annual rate were purchased at 30 times earnings and were sold 30 years later at 20 times earnings, an investor still would enjoy an average annual return of 18.4 percent (plus dividends). The 50 favored growth stocks became so popular with so many investors that they even were blessed with a nickname: the Nifty-Fifty. As a result of their popularity, the Nifty-Fifty eventually started selling at excessive PE ratios. According to *Fortune* magazine, in December 1972, the average PE ratio of the Nifty-Fifty growth stocks was 42 times. Coca-Cola sold at

46 times earnings, IBM at 35 times, Johnson & Johnson at 57 times, 3M at 39 times, Merck at 43 times, and Xerox at 46 times.

As it turned out, the Nifty-Fifty were not so nifty after all. The growth of most of the 50 slowed to normal or below-normal rates over the years. Worse, many of the companies developed serious problems. Two of the companies (Kodak and Polaroid) eventually filed for bankruptcy. A number of the other companies (including Digital Equipment and S. S. Kresge) ran into difficulties and were sold to larger companies at relatively low prices. It may be difficult to believe, but Citicorp (then named First National City Bank) was one of the Nifty-Fifty, as were J.C. Penney and Sears Roebuck.

At one time, the Nifty-Fifty were called one-decision stocks: a decision was made to purchase the stocks, and because the stocks would be held forever, no decision ever was required to sell them. Well, unfortunately for the advocates of the one-decision growth stocks, painful second decisions were required in 1973 when the prices of the Nifty-Fifty stocks started to tumble. From their 1973–1974 highs to their 1974 lows, the price of Xerox's shares declined by 71 percent, Avon's by 86 percent, and Polaroid's by 91 percent. The leading proponents of one-decision growth stocks had led their followers over a cliff.

It seems to me that the boom-bust of growth stocks in 1968–1974 and the subsequent boom-bust of Internet technology stocks in 1998–2002 serve to disprove the efficient market hypothesis, which states that it is impossible for an investor to beat the stock market because stocks always are efficiently priced based on all the relevant and known information on the fundamentals of the stocks. I believe that the efficient market hypothesis fails because it ignores human nature, particularly the nature of most individuals to be followers, not leaders.[1] As followers, humans are prone to embrace that which already has been faring well and to shun that which recently has been faring poorly. Of course, the act of buying into what already is doing well and shunning what is doing poorly serves to perpetuate a trend. Other trend followers then uncritically join the trend, causing the trend to feed on itself and causing excesses.

Often, investors invent a thesis to justify a trend: "Outsized returns can be realized by purchasing growth stocks regardless of their PE ratios because their PE ratios are not relevant over the longer term." Or "New Economy Internet stocks will continue to grow exponentially—and Old Economy stocks are dead and should be sold." In my opinion, booms become particularly dangerous when the theses that justify the booms generally become uncritically accepted by investors. Then, investors are prone to become complacent and to accept the excesses as new norms. History books are full of booms and busts, and booms and busts likely will continue to occur because of the proclivity of humans to become uncritical participants in trends and fads.

I have a thesis about why so many human beings are uncritical followers of trends. I cannot prove the thesis, but it makes sense to me. My experience and observations are that many intelligent investment professionals who are followers fully recognize that they are followers. Yet, try as they may, they do not have the innate ability to change and become leaders and buckers of the conventional wisdom. Thus, I conclude that their proclivity to be followers is at least partially, if not largely, hardwired and genetic. I further conclude that only a small percentage of humans are leaders. There is logic to this. Human beings have been civilized for only about 10,000 years. For the prior approximately 200,000 years, they were hunter-gatherers who traveled in bands in search of food and shelter. To be successful, bands normally could have only one leader. If there were more than one leader in a band, dissension likely would develop over decision making, and the stronger leader eventually would eliminate the weaker ones. Leaders tend to seek absolute power and sometimes will murder rivals or potential rivals in order to protect their position. History books tell of kings who murdered their siblings, or even their children, in order to eliminate the threat of competition. Thus, over tens of thousands of years, many humans with leadership genes were eliminated by survival of the fittest, leaving the vast majority of hunter-gatherers as followers. Scientists say that the genetic composition of present humans is almost identical to the genetic composition of hunter-gatherers. Therefore, only a minority of present humans have the leadership gene, and most humans tend to be followers.

A corollary thesis explains why so many investors are too focused on short-term fundamentals and investment returns at the expense of longer-term fundamentals and returns. Hunter-gatherers needed to be greatly concerned about their immediate survival—about a pride of lions that might be lurking behind the next rock or about the vicinity of a neighboring enemy tribe that might attack and kill. They did not have the luxury of thinking about longer-term planning. Through the selection process, many of those that did not possess the ability to react to immediate dangers did not survive. Then and today, humans often flinch when they come upon a sudden apparent danger—and, by definition, a flinch is instinctive as opposed to cognitive. Thus, over years, the selection process resulted in a subconscious proclivity for humans to be more concerned about the short term than the longer term.

I note that others also have come to the conclusion that much of human economic behavior is genetic. Notably, Daniel Kahneman won a Nobel Prize in 2002 for his work on prospect theory, which concludes that people often are prone to make irrational decisions that are based on inherited intuitions as opposed to logical conclusions. Kahneman and others invented a new branch of science called behavioral economics that studies the influence of human behavior on economic decision making.

Late in the 1998–2000 Internet boom, I received telephone calls from two clients who tended to be followers and who were overly focused on the short term. The first call was from Dick Albright, an intelligent older man who had sold his business and who now passionately collected antique Chinese furniture, especially furniture made from huanghuali wood. At the time Dick called, our stocks were doing fine, but not nearly as fine as Internet-related stocks. Dick mentioned that his son, who most unfortunately had lost his regular job and now was day-trading Internet stocks from a computer in his apartment, was materially outperforming Greenhaven. Dick strongly suggested that I test the waters by purchasing a few Internet stocks: "Just buy two or three to broaden your knowledge, because if you don't learn something about the New Economy, you may lose your relevance as an investment manager. Maybe my son can give you some ideas; maybe you can learn something from him about investing in the New Economy. Here is his telephone number. You really should call him; he is in his 20s and he really understands digital technology." I did not call him, and I did not purchase any of the overpriced Internet stocks.

The second call was from Frank Heat, a retired Goldman Sachs investment banking partner. Frank simply could not understand how Greenhaven managed to completely miss the Internet boom. "Where were you? Were you asleep?" I carefully explained what I normally explain to clients: that we are value investors who seek margins of safety in value stocks—and that there are risks of obsolescence in high-technology stocks that do not give us the margin of safety that we cherish.

Both clients called me several additional times with the same complaints. Finally, I successfully convinced Dick that he should seek another investment manager (maybe his otherwise unemployed son), and Frank left on his own accord. Of course, soon after the two clients departed (presumably for investment managers who were heavily invested in excessively priced New Economy Internet stocks), the bubble abruptly burst, with many technology stocks losing more than three-quarters of their market value.

During the 1997–2000 boom period for technology stocks, a typical Greenhaven account's average annual return was 18.5 percent. The Standard & Poor's (S&P) 500 Index's average annual return during the period was 22.4 percent (the Index was heavily weighted with technology stocks). We lagged. Near the end of the boom, I was happy to lag. I told my associates that if the S&P 500 Index continued to increase sharply due to the further appreciation of materially overvalued Internet-related stocks, I wanted to lag the Index. The only way we could outperform an already overvalued index was to take risks that would be unwise, unsound, and irresponsible.

Then, during the sharp market decline of 2001 and 2002, Greenhaven's average annual return was a positive 3.4 percent, while the S&P 500's was a negative 18.2 percent. Internet and many other New Economy technology stocks were dumped by investors. Our stocks generally held their own, in spite of the strong headwind of a declining stock market.

Every once in a while, the stars align for an investment manager. Such was the case in 2003 to 2005. In early 2003, the "Old Economy" stocks we owned were selling at undeservedly depressed prices. They had been underowned during the Internet boom. Furthermore, we had an exciting opportunity to purchase shares of companies that produce commodities. In the early 2000s, China and a number of other emerging countries markedly increased the quantities of crude oil, steel, copper, and other commodities they were purchasing to meet the needs of their growing economies. Demand started to exceed supply for many commodities, and their prices started to rise sharply. Greenhaven noticed this and purchased shares of companies that produce oil, fertilizer, and paper. We were in the right place at the right time, and during the three-year period 2003 through 2005, our average annual return was 34 percent, far above the S&P 500's 12.8 percent.

I sometimes wonder how Dick Albright's and Frank Heat's portfolios fared during the 2000–2005 period. Probably quite poorly. Patience, steady emotions, and common sense all are important attributes when investing in common stocks.

The sharp increase in commodity prices between 2003 and 2008 helped create an opportunity for us to purchase Whirlpool's shares in 2011 at a particularly and undeservedly depressed price. The years 2003 through 2011 were an absolutely hellish period for Whirlpool. From 2003 to 2011 the price of steel, copper, and plastics (the key raw materials used to manufacture appliances) increased sharply. The price of copper increased from an average of $0.81 per pound in 2003 to about $4 per pound in 2011. During the same eight-year period, the typical domestic price of hot rolled steel increased from about $270 per ton to about $650 per ton. Between 2003 and 2011, Whirlpool's annual raw materials costs increased by about $3.5 billion, or by about 18 percent of revenues. What a headwind! Actually, what a storm! Moreover, after the housing market started to weaken in 2007, the demand for large appliances fell sharply. According to the Association of Home Appliance Manufactures, U.S. industry sales of the "big 6" appliances (washers, dryers, refrigerators, freezers, dishwashers, and ranges) declined from about 47 million units in 2006 to about 36 million in 2011. In an environment of weak demand, Whirlpool had difficulties increasing prices sufficiently to offset its increased costs for raw materials. Thus, Whirlpool simultaneously suffered from increased raw material costs, reduced sales, and pressured pricing. Not a happy situation.

Amazingly, Whirlpool remained profitable during the entire 2003–2011 period in spite of the hurricane-force headwinds. To the credit of management (especially Jeff Fettig, who had become CEO in 2004), the company aggressively and continually reduced its costs during the period. Products were redesigned to reduce the use of raw materials and to increase the commonality of parts, plants were consolidated and relocated to low-cost geographies, employee benefits were reduced, and advertising and other overhead expenditures were curtailed. In Whirlpool's 2008 annual report, management listed three strategic priorities. The first priority on the list was to "reduce our global cost structure":

We are taking aggressive action to redesign our products with global standards for parts and components. This proven global approach lowers costs, improves quality, and speeds our time from design to market. The difficult decision to close five manufacturing facilities and reduce approximately 5,000 positions globally will allow us to further reduce costs and operate more efficiently in 2009. We are aggressively managing all costs in every part of our business to rapidly adjust our cost structure to current and expected global demand levels. … The decisive and thoughtful actions we are taking today will significantly lower our overall cost structure.

In the spring of 2011, Greenhaven studied Whirlpool's fundamentals. We immediately were impressed by management's ability and willingness to slash costs. In spite of a materially subnormal demand for appliances in 2010, the company was able to earn operating margins of 5.9 percent. Often, when a company is suffering from particularly adverse industry conditions, it is unable to earn any profit at all. But Whirlpool remained moderately profitable. If the company could earn 5.9 percent margins under adverse circumstances, what could the company earn once the U.S. housing market and the appliance market returned to normal?

We made an Excel model that guesstimated what Whirlpool might earn in 2016. The model assumed that the housing industry had recovered by then. About 53 percent of Whirlpool's revenues came from the United States. The remaining revenues came from Latin America (mostly Brazil), Europe, and Asia (mostly India). We made conservative guesses about future non-U.S. revenues and profit margins, but focused most of our efforts trying to project future U.S. earnings. Our best guess was that if the housing industry recovered, U.S. revenues would grow at a 7 to 8 percent CAGR between 2010 and 2016. We then tried to analyze Whirlpool's operating leverage. After looking at past data and after speaking to management, we estimated that for each $1 increase in revenues, Whirlpool's pretax profits should increase by about $0.20 before future cost reductions (and the company was in the midst of several programs to further reduce costs). Our conclusion was that the company's revenues and operating margins in 2016 could be roughly $25 billion and 10 percent, and thus its operating profits could be about $2,500 million. We estimated that the company's 2016 interest costs, effective tax rate, and diluted share count would be $275 million, 28 percent, and 80 million, respectively. Given these educated guesses and projections, Whirlpool would earn about $20 per share in 2016.

The $20 earnings per share (EPS) estimate assumed that raw material costs stabilized but did not decline. My analysis was that there was a high probability that the prices of steel and copper actually would decline between 2011 and 2016, thereby providing Whirlpool with an additional tailwind. The price of copper, for example, started spiking sharply in 2003. The apparent primary cause of its fivefold increase in price by 2011 was China. The numbers are telling. Between 2003 and 2011, China's consumption of copper increased at a 12.4 percent annual rate from 3,056,000 tons to 7,815,000 tons. In 2011, China consumed 4 out of every 10 pounds of copper consumed in the world.

My experience and logic is that when the price of a commodity increases sharply, countervailing forces come into play. Specifically, high prices incentivize producers to increase their capacity and incentivize users to reduce their consumption through conservation or substitution (aluminum can replace copper in many electrical applications). There is elasticity of supply and elasticity of demand. The usual result is that supplies start exceeding demands—and, consistent with the laws of supply and demand, prices fall.

Over the years, when an industry's condition turns tight, I have often heard management say "it is different this time; the industry has become disciplined and will not add excess capacity." However, except for commodities whose supplies and prices are controlled by cartels, I have yet to witness a commodity that has remained in tight supply for a prolonged period. It takes only one or two managements who desire to add capacity in order to take advantage of existing highly profitable conditions. Then, other managements, fearful of losing market share, also start planning capacity additions. The result is large additions to capacity and a resulting softer (or soft) market. Unless pricing is controlled by a cartel, commodities tend to be cyclical—very cyclical.

The proclivity of managements to develop herd instincts when deciding to add to capacity is an example of the "fallacy of composition," which states that a decision or action that is rational for one or a few individuals or companies becomes irrational if a whole group of individuals or companies follow the decision or action, and the outcome of the irrationality is adverse for all. An example of the fallacy of composition would be the tendency of hundreds of theatergoers to simultaneously rush for the single exit when there is a cry of "fire" in a crowded theater. If only a few had rushed for an exit, they likely would have made a quick, unharmed escape. But the simultaneous rush of hundreds likely would result in trampling and injuries, or worse.

I was a witness to one decision to add to capacity. In 1981, I received a telephone call from Bob Hellendale, the chairman and president of Great Northern Nekoosa Corporation, a manufacturer of newsprint, pulp, and other "paper" products. Great Northern was considering constructing a large new pulp mill on the Leaf River in Mississippi. Bob Hellendale planned to present the plans to Great Northern's board of directors for approval, and he asked me to listen to and critique his presentation prior to the board meeting. The economics of the proposed mill largely were a function of the cost of the mill, investment tax credits that Great Northern would receive from the U.S. government, the assumed price of pulp, and the assumed production and overhead costs. Bob Hellendale's projections assumed that prices would increase at a rate near the top end of their historical range and that costs would increase near the bottom end. It seemed to me that Great Northern's management wanted to build the mill and had adopted assumptions that would justify the construction. When Greenhaven is weighing whether or not to purchase a security, we usually make assumptions that hopefully will prove conservative. Great Northern did just the opposite. So much for discipline within an industry that produces commodities!

A securities analyst or portfolio manager must be careful when basing decisions on statistical information, such as historical price or cost trends. Statistics can be misleading if they are incomplete or are slanted to justify a predetermined decision, such as the decision to build the pulp mill. An example of a misleading statistic is the statistician who relied on his conclusion that a stream was three feet deep on average—and drowned trying to cross it.

Now that we had concluded that Whirlpool could earn as much as $20 per share in 2016 if the housing industry fully recovered by then, we had to value the shares. This proved to be difficult. While I have spent most of my working life valuing companies, sometimes I am stumped because of uncertainties. In the case of Whirlpool, I had difficulty assessing the company's competitive position. It appeared that the company was the low-cost producer in its industry and that most of its competitors were unprofitable. There were several other positives: Whirlpool had eliminated a major competitor when it purchased Maytag; Sears Roebuck appeared to be losing market share (and in trouble as a company); and GE seemed to have lost some of its competitiveness due to insufficient investments in productivity and design. But there also was a large negative. Two Korean competitors (LG and Samsung) seemed bent on gaining market share, even if they needed to slash prices to do so. Whirlpool had filed antidumping charges against the Korean companies, but the outcomes of the charges were uncertain. On balance, my best guess was that Whirlpool was not worth more than 15 times its normalized earnings, but likely was worth more than 12 times its earnings, and therefore that the shares might be worth $250 to $300 in 2016. However, I finally decided that my current valuation made little difference. If Whirlpool came close to earning $20 per share in 2016, the shares (which were selling at about $80 in the spring of 2011) would be an exciting investment regardless of whether they were worth 15 times earnings or 12 times earnings or even 10 times earnings. My plan was to aggressively purchase the shares and then have plenty of time over the next few years to refine both my earnings estimate and my valuation. When you think you are hitting a home run, you need not dwell on whether the ball is likely to end up in the lower deck, the upper deck, or out of the ball park—and I did not have to dwell over valuing Whirlpool's shares to know that they were an exciting investment opportunity. After a moderate amount of further due diligence and after reading a few Wall Street reports on Whirlpool, I started purchasing the company's shares.

I should note that, in 2011, Wall Street analysts generally were not positive about Whirlpool's shares. The analysts were focused largely on the company's short-term problems to the exclusion of the company's longer-term potential. A report by J. P. Morgan dated April 27, 2011, stated that Whirlpool's current share price properly reflected the company's increased costs for raw materials, the company's inability to increase its prices, and the current soft demand for appliances. J. P. Morgan maintained its "neutral" rating on the shares.

The J. P. Morgan report might have been correct about the near-term outlook for Whirlpool and its shares. But Greenhaven invests with a two- to four-year time horizon and cares little about the near-term outlook for its holdings. We knew that Whirlpool's shares might remain flat or even decline before they appreciated, but any temporary flatness or decline in the price of the shares would not affect the final return on our investment. I viewed Whirlpool's shares as an abnormally fat pitch. Should a batter let an abnormally fat pitch go by with hopes that a future pitch will be even fatter? I think not. In fact, I believed there was a high probability that the short-term problems detailed by J. P. Morgan and others likely were already largely or fully discounted into the price of the share, and therefore were the opportunity.

I was particularly excited about Whirlpool's shares because they had the potential to increase several-fold over the next few years if the wind happened to blow in the right direction. For example, if the housing industry started to improve sharply in the near future and if the prices of steel and copper started to decline, it would not have been unreasonable to estimate that Whirlpool could earn about $15 per share in 2014 and that its shares could then roughly triple in price (to roughly $240, or 16 times earnings) between 2011 and 2014. I have noticed that, over the years, a disproportionately large percentage of Greenhaven's returns have come from relatively few of its holdings. In fact, I would make an even stronger statement: a relatively modest percentage of our holdings have been responsible for the bulk of our success since our founding in 1987. Greenhaven's stretch goal is to achieve average annual returns of 20 percent for its clients (because 20 percent is a stretch, we generally say that our goal is 15 to 20 percent). If one in five of our holdings triples in value over a three-year period, then the other four holdings only have to achieve 12 percent average annual returns in order for our entire portfolio to achieve its stretch goal of 20 percent. For this reason, Greenhaven works extra hard trying to identify potential multibaggers. Whirlpool had the potential to be a multibagger because it was selling at a particularly low multiple of its potential earnings power. Of course, most of our potential multibaggers do not turn out to be multibaggers. But one cannot hit a multibagger unless one tries, and sometimes our holdings that initially appear to be less exciting eventually benefit from positive unforeseen events (handsome black swans) and unexpectedly turn out to be a complete winner. For this reason, we like to remain fully invested as long as our holdings remain reasonably priced and free from large risks of permanent loss. I am continually reminded of a favorite saying of Mr. Arthur Ross (my old boss who liked to say everything twice): "stay in the game, Ed, stay in the game."

We purchased a sizable position in Whirlpool in the first half of 2011 at a time when the shares were selling at about $80. In the second half of 2011, the appliance market and Whirlpool's earnings were disappointing, and the shares traded down to as low as about $50. When shares of one of our holdings are weak, we ask ourselves a question: are the reasons we purchased the shares still valid (and thus the weakness attributable to a temporary problem), or was our original analysis and judgment flawed? If we believe that our original analysis and judgment was correct, then we often will take advantage of the weakness and purchase additional shares. If, however, we come to the conclusion that our original analysis and judgment was faulty, we usually will admit to our error and sell our holding in the shares, hopefully before the loss becomes large. We realize that from time to time we will make mistakes. If we never made a mistake, we should be properly criticized for being too conservative. To make money, one must take some risks. The question is where one should draw the line on risks. There is no single correct answer to this question because different investors have different investment objectives, different balance sheets, and different emotional tolerances to risk.

We gradually added to our holding in Whirlpool in the second half of 2011 and into 2012. During 2012, I continued to monitor the opinions of Wall Street analysts, particularly those at J. P. Morgan and Goldman Sachs. Neither firm had adopted our thesis on Whirlpool's attractiveness. J. P. Morgan remained "neutral" on the stock during 2011 and 2012. On February 1, 2012, a Goldman Sachs report estimated that Whirlpool would earn only $4.56 in 2012 and $5.97 in 2014. The report recommended that the shares be sold, even though they were selling at only $62 at the time, or at only 10.4 times the firm's estimate of 2014 earnings. On October 23, 2012, Whirlpool announced favorable earnings for the

September quarter, increased its EPS guidance for 2012 to $6.90 to $7.10, and publicly stated: "We have delivered three consecutive quarters of year-over-year operating margin improvement this year. … Our ongoing business performance should continue to improve due to our strong cadence of new product innovations, the benefit of our cost savings programs, and positive trends in U.S. housing." The following day, Goldman Sachs increased its 2012 EPS estimate to $7.09 and changed its opinion of the shares from a "sell" to a "buy." On the day the Goldman report was issued, the shares sold at $94, up more than 50 percent from nine months earlier when Goldman recommended selling the shares.

The year 2013 was a breakout year for Whirlpool. Housing starts in the United States increased by 18 percent to 925,000, domestic sales of the "big 6" appliances grew by 9.5 percent, and Whirlpool's EPS increased by 42 percent to $10.02. Reacting to the good news, the price of the shares increased by 54 percent, from $101.76 at the start of the year to $156.86 at year-end. One robin does not make a spring, but now there were several robins on Whirlpool's lawn. I was excited that we had doubled our money in the shares, and I was excited that our thesis on housing-related stocks appeared to be working.

During the spring of 2014, I heard rumors that Whirlpool might be interested in acquiring Indesit, a European manufacturer of appliances that had put itself up for sale. I immediately wrote a letter to Jeff Fettig (Whirlpool's chairman and CEO) suggesting that Whirlpool not acquire Indesit. Whirlpool had a bright future. It did not need to make an acquisition. An acquisition would leverage the balance sheet and distract management. Europe was a tough place to do business. Many acquisitions do not turn out as planned. The sellers know more than the buyers and may know of problems or uncertainties that are not apparent to the buyers. Jeff answered me with a "form" letter that stated that Whirlpool would acquire Indesit only if the acquisition made sense for the shareholders. What else could he say?

In July, Whirlpool announced an agreement to acquire Indesit for $2 billion. Chris, Josh, and I immediately telephoned Jeff. He calmed us. Indesit had revenues of $3.5 billion, so the company was being acquired for only 0.57 times revenues. There would be about $350 million of synergies (equal to more than $3 per share after taxes) when Whirlpool's European operations were combined with Indesit's. Two head offices would be combined into one. Plants would be consolidated. Increased purchasing power should lead to lower prices for purchased parts. Efficiencies would be gained through best practices. Research and design would be consolidated. Furthermore, about $1.4 billion of the revenues were from Russia and Eastern Europe, where long-term growth prospects were strong. In 2013, Whirlpool's European operations only broke even. Jeff's best guess was that when the synergies were fully realized in about 2017, the European operations should have 7 to 8 percent operating margins on well over $7 billion of revenues. We thanked Jeff for his time and put a pencil to his estimates, realizing that he had a vested interest in making the acquisition appear attractive. Seven to 8 percent margins on $7 to $8 billion of revenues would result in $490 to $640 million of operating earnings. A 4 percent interest rate on $2 billion of additional borrowings to pay for the acquisition would increase annual interest expense by $80 million. Thus, if Jeff's projections happened to be correct, Whirlpool's European operations would contribute $410 to $560 million to pretax profits in 2017, or $3.70 to $5 per share after taxes at a 28 percent effective rate and based on 80 million shares outstanding. Whirlpool was taking a risk, but the risk appeared worth taking. I regretted having written the negative letter to Jeff. I had jumped the gun.

Whirlpool also made a smaller acquisition in 2014: a 51 percent interest in Hefei Sanyo, a Chinese manufacturer and distributor of appliances. Hefei sold $862 million of appliances in 2013 through about 30,000 distributors. Whirlpool had only 3,000 distributors in China. By acquiring the 51 percent controlling interest, Whirlpool could market its line of appliances through Hefei's thousands of distributors, thus hopefully materially expanding its revenues in China from a very small base. Jeff Fettig believed that Hefei's revenues could grow at a 15 to 25 percent rate and that its operating margins could be 8 to 10 percent. Assuming growth at a 20 percent rate and margins at 9 percent, Hefei would contribute about

$0.60 per share to Whirlpool's 2016 EPS—not a game changer, but a material addition to earnings in a large and rapidly growing country.

At the time we originally purchased our shares in Whirlpool, we had one concept: the company and its shares would benefit from the recovery of the housing market. Now, we had an additional concept: Whirlpool had a smart and ambitious management that was finding ways to grow the company. This was an important concept because if the company could grow over the longer term at a rate materially faster than the appliance industry, it was worth a higher multiple of earnings. I had originally valued Whirlpool at 12 to 15 times earnings. Now, I was beginning to believe that the company might be worth materially more than 15 times. Thus, it increasingly appeared to us that our investment in Whirlpool's shares could appreciate several fold versus our cost basis—and thus make a lot of money for our clients and us. And, equally important, we would enjoy the psychological satisfaction of knowing that our theses on the company and on the housing market had proven correct. In the end, the psychological rewards of being right can be as important as—or more important than the monetary rewards. And they are interrelated. When you feel good, you are more likely to do well.

NOTE

1. Other human traits that cause the efficient market theory to fail include the proclivities of many investors to be influenced by biases or by emotional impulses. Emotions are an enemy of strong performance in the stock market.

11

BOEING

When I become interested in a company, I usually like to read about the company's history. Who started the company—and why and how? How did the company's industry come into being? Histories can be informative, interesting, and sometimes entertaining. The way I look at it, the holdings in our portfolios are my career's family members—and I would never agreeably marry a girlfriend without first learning about her background and meeting her parents.

From the earliest days of recorded history, we have evidence of man's interest in flight, especially the flight of birds. If birds could fly, why couldn't man? Imaginations ran. In Greek mythology, Daedalus used wax to attach wings of bird feathers to his son Icarus. Daedalus's device worked, until Icarus disobediently flew too close to the sun, with exceedingly ill consequences when the sun's heat melted the wax. Many centuries later, in 852 A.D., one Armen Firman tried to mimic a bird in flight. He constructed two wings out of vulture feathers, attached the wings to his arms, "flew" out of a tower in Cordoba (Spain), and promptly crash landed, injuring his back in the process. Then, in 1010, an English monk tried flying from a tower in the Abbey of Malmesbury. He broke both legs. Not to be deterred, in 1496 a man named Seccio attempted to fly from a tower in Nuremberg (Germany). He broke both arms. Thus, wax fasteners and tower jumping did little to advance the flight of human beings.

Leonardo da Vinci did advance the science of flight. After studying the flight of birds, he designed a number of possible flying machines, including types of gliders, rotorcrafts, and parachutes. In 1496, da Vinci actually built a glider. However, the glider never was tested, so human flight continued to remain an unfulfilled dream.

The dream advanced in the early seventeenth century when Galileo proved that air has weight. If air has weight, then man could fabricate a hollow sphere out of lightweight material, pump the air out of the sphere, and thus create a lighter than air vehicle that could rise into the sky. Such a vehicle was called a balloon. It is difficult to form a vacuum inside a balloon made out of lightweight material, but if the inside of the balloon were filled with hot air (which is lighter than room temperature air), man finally could build a device that could fly. On August 8, 1708, Bartolomeu de Gusmao, a Brazilian priest, made a small balloon out of paper, placed the open end of the balloon over a fire, and, with members of the Portuguese royalty in audience, watched as the balloon lifted into the air by more than 10 feet.

Balloon technology developed slowly for the next 75 years, but then accelerated sharply in 1783, which was a breakout year for the success and popularity of lighter-than-air flights. On June 4, 1783, the French brothers Joseph and Jacques Montgolfier, who owned a paper mill, held a flame under a large silk-lined paper balloon and, in front of a large crowd of onlookers, watched as the balloon lifted by more than 6,000 feet into the air. Then, on September 19, the Montgolfiers flew a hot air balloon carrying a sheep, a rooster, and a duck for eight minutes at Versailles in front of King Louis XVI, Marie Antoinette, much of the French court, and a crowd of tens of thousands of curious onlookers.

At the same time that the Montgolfiers were hard at work with their hot air balloons, French Professor Jacques Charles, along with the Roberts brothers, were busy designing and building a hydrogen balloon. In 1766,

Henry Cavendish discovered hydrogen, which is lighter than air. Jacques Charles believed that hydrogen balloons would be vastly superior to hot air balloons. But first, a gas-tight material had to be invented. This happened when Jacques Charles and the two Roberts developed a gas-tight rubberized silk, made by dissolving rubber in turpentine and then varnishing the solution on a sheet of silk. In August 1783, Jacques Charles and the Robert brothers fabricated a rubberized silk balloon, filled the balloon with hydrogen, and released it from the Champ de Mars in Paris, now the site of the Eiffel Tower. A large crowd, which included Benjamin Franklin, was on hand for the release. When untethered, the balloon rose and headed north, followed by dozens of chasers on horseback. When the balloon landed 13 miles away in the village of Gonesse, local villagers were so terrified of the strange, alien looking object that they attacked it with pitchforks, which became an inglorious end to a glorious and historic flight.

Now that a sheep, a duck, and a rooster had flown, the Montgolfiers were anxious to launch a manned flight. On October 19, in a test flight, three Frenchman successfully rose into the air in a balloon that remained tethered to the ground. Next, it was time for a manned free flight. At first, King Louis XVI suggested that condemned criminals should be the guinea pigs for the dangerous first free flight, but the scientist Jean-Francois Pilatre de Rozier and the Marquis Francois d'Arlandes successfully volunteered to be the pioneers. On November 21, a balloon carrying the two Frenchman lifted off from the center of Paris, rose to an altitude of about 500 feet, and drifted about 5 miles in 20 minutes before landing. The manned flight was considered an historic event that excited the spectators. Benjamin Franklin, after witnessing the flight, wrote in his diary: "We observed it lift off in the most majestic manner. When it reached around 250 feet in altitude, the intrepid voyagers lowered their hats to salute the spectators. We could not help feeling a certain mixture of awe and admiration."

After the November 21 manned flight, a balloon craze swept through France. Dinner plates were decorated with pictures of balloons, as were chairs and the dial of clocks. Balloons became the talk of the town and throughout much of Europe.

The hot air and hydrogen balloons of the late eighteenth and early nineteenth centuries were interesting and popular novelties, but largely were impractical because they depended on winds to float from one locality to another. A breakthrough came in 1852 when Henry Giffard designed a nonrigid, steerable hydrogen airship that was powered by a 3-horsepower steam engine attached to a three-bladed propeller. On September 24, Giffard made the first powered and controlled air flight in a 17-mile trip from Paris to Trappes. But it was inconvenient to have a steam engine aboard an airship, and a 3-horsepower engine was not powerful enough to buck winds any stronger than a breeze. Thus, the Giffard airship was an advance but not a solution to air travel.

Over the next few decades, progress toward pragmatic manned flight was slow but steady. One advance came in 1884 when a French army captain and colonel flew the electric-powered La France airship (now called a dirigible) at four miles per hour in a five-mile loop that included an upwind leg as well as a downwind leg. The La France's 8.5-horsepower electric engine was powered by chlorochromic batteries that weighed about 1,000 pounds. Because of the heavy weight and limited capacity of the batteries, the La France was not the answer to commercial manned flight.

In 1872, Paul Haenlein, a German engineer, designed a 164-foot-long dirigible that was powered by an internal combustion engine attached to a propeller that was 15 feet in diameter. The engine was fueled by coal gas. On December 13, Haenlein's dirigible was successfully tested at Brunn, Germany. Other tests of dirigibles powered by internal combustion engines continued in the 1880s and 1890s. By the late 1890s, it became clear that commercially successful steerable dirigibles powered by internal combustion engines someday could be designed and produced. But, as the nineteenth century came to a close, to quote from a Robert Frost poem, the sky "at least this far, for all the fuss of the populace, stays more popular than populous."

Then, in the early 1900s, Count Ferdinand Zeppelin successfully tested a 385-foot-long steerable dirigible that could travel at a speed of close to 20 miles per hour for several hundred miles at an altitude of several thousand feet. The count had become interested in the concept of manned air travel in 1874 after hearing a lecture on the possible use of dirigibles to carry mail. After retiring from the army in 1890, the count went to work designing a rigid frame air ship that was durable and reliable. The first "zeppelin" was tested in Germany over Lake Constance on July 2, 1890. While the first test and many subsequent tests were aborted due to problems, by 1909 the zeppelin was ready for commercial flights. The count then formed an airline (popularly called DELAG) and started offering pleasure cruises for up to 20 adventurous passengers at a time. Commercial aviation was born.

However, the use of zeppelins for air travel soon was eclipsed by the commercialization of heavier-than-air flight. While many scientists contributed to understanding how heavier-than-air vehicles someday could fly commercially, many believe that Sir George Cayley, the sixth Baronet of Brompton, is the true father of the airplane. Born to wealth in 1773, Sir Cayley became an inventor and engineer. He is credited with inventing self-righting lifeboats, automatic signals for railway crossings, seat belts, an internal combustion engine fueled by gunpowder, and several types of "flying machines." His most important aeronautical achievements include a scientific understanding of how birds fly; a clarification of how a cambered airfoil could provide sufficient lift to offset gravity; an improved understanding of thrust and drag; and the design of gliders that included wings, fuselages, and tails with horizontal stabilizers and vertical fins. In 1848, he built and tested a glider large enough to carry a child, and five years later, he built a glider large enough to carry a full-sized man. The first manned glider flight took place on a sloped meadow at Brompton Dale, which was about a mile from Cayley's Brompton Hall estate. The glider was carried to the top of the slope, a "pilot" (one of Cayley's coachmen) climbed into the craft, and then workmen grabbed ropes that were attached to the craft and started hauling it down the slope until it lifted into the air. The glider flew about 600 feet across a small valley before it crash-landed.

Sir Cayley had helped prove that a fixed cambered wing attached to a fuselage could provide sufficient lift to fly human beings through the air. Now, if engine-driven propellers could be used to provide the thrust needed to drive the gliders forward, gliders could become airplanes. In 1896, Samuel Pierpont Langley, an American scientist and inventor, designed such an airplane, which he named the Aerodrome #5. Langley was born in Roxbury, Massachusetts, in 1834. He attended Boston Latin School where, at the age of 9, he started reading books on astronomy. After false starts as an apprentice architect and a telescope maker, Langley accepted a job as an assistant at Harvard College's observatory. This led to subsequent jobs at other observatories where he researched and advanced the science of astronomy. In 1886, he was awarded a medal from the National Academy of Sciences for his contribution to solar physics, especially to the understanding of sunspots. A year later, he was appointed the third secretary of the Smithsonian Institution, which was an honor as well as a recognition of his abilities.

In the 1880s, Langley developed an interest in aeronautics. He first experimented with aircraft that were powered by rubber bands, but he soon abandoned rubber bands in favor of small steam engines. On May 6, 1896, Langley placed Aerodrome #5, which was powered by a steam engine and was unmanned, on top of a houseboat that was anchored on the Potomac River near Quantico, Virginia. To provide a requisite initial thrust, #5 was attached to a spring-actuated catapult. When the catapult was released, #5 flew more than 3,000 feet at a speed of about 25 miles per hour before landing in the river. A second test on May 6 also was successful. Then, on November 28, Aerodrome #6, also unmanned, flew about 5,000 feet. The November 28 test was witnessed and photographed by Alexander Graham Bell. Buoyed by these successes and their favorable publicity, Langley moved full speed ahead, and with funding from the U.S. government, he designed and successfully tested aerodromes that were powered by 52-horsepower internal combustion engines. Finally, after several years of design and testing, Langley was ready for a manned test of an aerodrome. On October 7, 1903, Charles M. Manley, a Cornell-educated mechanical engineer, attempted to pilot the aerodrome off the anchored houseboat, but a wing clipped the catapult, and the plane plummeted into the Potomac. Luckily, pilot Manley was not injured. Then, on

December 8, Manley climbed into the aerodrome for a second test. This time, the plane broke apart just after leaving the catapult. Again, Manley escaped injury. Upon study, Langley concluded that the aerodrome was too fragile for a 52-horsepower engine.

Nine days after the second aerodrome crash, the Wright brothers successfully flew the Kitty Hawk Flyer 1 at Kitty Hawk, North Carolina—and history was made. Wilbur (1867–1912) and Orville (1871–1948) Wright were born in the Midwest at a time when the industrial revolution sparked unusual interest in science and experimentation. In 1878, the boys' father brought home a toy helicopter for his sons to play with. The helicopter was about a foot long and was made of paper, bamboo, and cork. A rubber band powered its rotor. The boys were fascinated with the helicopter and played with it until it broke. Then, they built a replica. Years later, Wilbur and Orville claimed that the toy helicopter sparked their interest in flight.

Wilbur and Orville both attended, but did not complete, high school. Orville dropped out of school in 1889 to design his own printing press, and soon the entrepreneurial brothers started publishing a weekly newspaper, the *West Side News*, with Wilbur as editor. Three years later, the brothers became interested in the bicycle craze that was sweeping the nation soon after the invention of the modern "safety bike." The brothers opened a bicycle sales and repair shop in Dayton, Ohio, and later started manufacturing their own brand under the name of the Wright Cycle Company. Then, in the late 1890s, intrigued by newspaper reports of Langley's experiments with flying, the brothers became interested in designing an airplane of their own. In May 1899, Wilbur wrote a letter to the Smithsonian Institution requesting publications and information on airplanes. Then, using the discoveries of da Vinci, Cayley, Langley, and others, the brothers started designing an airplane. From the start, the Wright brothers were convinced that existing knowledge of lift and thrust was adequate for successful flights, but that the problems of controlling flights had not been solved. Based on observations of birds and bicycles, the brothers came up with the notion that airplanes should bank during turns. This notion led to the design of wings that could change shapes, thereby permitting aircraft to roll into turns. They also invented other methods and devices that allowed pilots to control flights, such as using rudders to eliminate adverse yaw. With their new methods for controlling flight, between mid-1900 and the fall of 1902, the brothers conducted more than 700 tests with gliders. The hundreds of successful tests convinced the brothers that they were now ready to build a powered aircraft. In early 1903, the Flyer 1 was built and tested in a wind tunnel. After a failed search to purchase an efficient lightweight motor for the Flyer, the brothers asked their shop mechanic, Charlie Taylor, to build an engine. The Taylor engine was rated at 12 horsepower, far less than the 52-horsepower engine that proved too powerful for Samuel Langley's aerodrome.

By December, the Flyer was ready to fly. With Wilbur as pilot, an attempted flight was made on December 13, but the engine immediately stalled and the plane flew for only three seconds. After repair of minor damage, another attempt was made on December 17. At 10:30 a.m., with Orville at the controls, the Flyer successfully flew 120 feet in 12 seconds. The flight was witnessed by five people, including John Daniels, who photographed the plane in flight. Three other manned fights were conducted that day, with Orville and Wilbur taking turns as pilots. The fourth flight covered 852 feet in 59 seconds. The Wright brothers were to become famous.

Between 1904 and 1908, the brothers worked on improving the reliability and mobility of their planes. A major advancement came in August 1908, when Wilbur made a series of technically challenging flights, including figure eights, at the Hunaudieres horse-racing track near Le Mans, France. Thousands came to witness the flights. The French originally were skeptical of the Wrights' achievements, but after the demonstrations at Hunaudieres, the French treated the brothers as heroes. Louis Bleriot, a leading French aviator, wrote: "For a long time, the Wright brothers have been accused in Europe of bluff … but today they are hallowed in France." The Wright brothers, and aviation in general, had become front-page news.

For the next several years, there was a constant parade of firsts. In 1909, a woman (Baroness de la Roche) learned to fly. In 1910, a U.S. Navy pilot flew a Curtis plane off the deck of a ship. Also in 1910, Henri Fabre became the first to fly a floatplane. In 1912, Harriet Quimby flew across the English Channel in a Bleriot monoplane. And in 1914, the first aerial combat occurred when Allied and German pilots fired at each other with pistols and rifles (all without much effect).

On July 4, 1914, a flight took place in Seattle, Washington, that had a major effect on the history of aviation. On that day, a barnstormer named Terah Maroney was hired to perform a flying demonstration as part of Seattle's Independence Day celebrations. After displaying aerobatics in his Curtis floatplane, Maroney landed and offered to give free rides to spectators. One spectator, William Edward Boeing, a wealthy owner of a lumber company, quickly accepted Maroney's offer. Boeing was so exhila-rated by the flight that he completely caught the aviation bug—a bug that was to be with him for the rest of his life.

William Boeing was born in Detroit in 1881 to Mary and Wilhelm Boeing. Wilhelm, who had immigrated to the United States from Germany at the age of 20, became a wealthy owner and operator of timberlands. Young William spent most of his adolescence at Swiss boarding schools. He then studied at Yale, but left before graduating in order to start a log-ging company of his own in Grays Harbor, Washington.

Boeing had first become interested in airplanes when he attended an air show in Los Angeles in 1910. Upon returning from the air show to his home in Seattle, he approached a friend, George Conrad Westervelt, a naval officer and engineer who had studied aeronautics at MIT, about the possibility of building an airplane. The discussions initially were pre-liminary in nature. However, after Boeing's ride with Maroney in 1914, the discussions became serious and led to a decision to enter the business of manufacturing airplanes. Westervelt would design a single-engine float-plane, and Boeing would provide the financing and the "manufacturing plant," which initially was a boathouse on Lake Union owned by Boeing. In 1915, Westervelt went to work designing a plane and Boeing went to California to take flying lessons from Glenn Martin, a pioneer aviator. The first Westervelt-designed aircraft, a two-seat floatplane called the B&W,

was ready to fly by late spring 1916. On June 15, with William Boeing at the controls, the plane taxied across part of Lake Union, picked up speed, and lifted majestically into the sky. The inaugural flight, as well as subsequent flights later in June, confirmed that the plane was a technological success. By July, Boeing was ready to start producing B&W planes in mass. He formed a company called Pacific Aero Products Company to build and market the planes. The U.S. Navy was an obvious early prospect for B&Ws, but the Navy turned Boeing down, instead opting to stick with the more proven Curtis floatplanes. Undeterred, Boeing finally sold two planes to the New Zealand Flying School. Pacific Aero Products (which was renamed the Boeing Airplane Company in 1917) was in business.

During the early days of aeronautics, improvements came rapidly. In late 1916, Boeing designed an improved floatplane, which it called the Model C. The Model C was ready to be marketed in April 1917, the same month that the United States entered World War I. Boeing believed that the Navy now might need training aircraft. He was correct. The Navy ordered two Model Cs that were shipped to the Naval Air Station in Pensacola, Florida. The planes performed so well that the Navy ordered 50 more. The order put Boeing on the map.

Boeing's business flourished during the war, but predictably fell off sharply after the armistice. The company responded to the fall-off by designing a plane for commercial use. Fishing enthusiasts were interested in accessing the many isolated lakes in the Northwest United States. Boeing designed a small floatplane (called the B-1) to satisfy this need, but initially only a few were purchased. Interest in aeronautics had waned after the end of World War I.

However, interest in air flights quickly accelerated after Charles Lindberg's highly publicized 1927 transatlantic flight in the *Spirit of St. Louis,* and Boeing eventually was able to sell 13 of the B-1s. Thirteen is not a large number, but was a respectable number for the era because in the 1920s, air travel remained an uncomfortable novelty. Airplane fuselages were thin sheets of uninsulated metal that often rattled. Passengers often stuck cotton in their ears to dampen the noise of the engines. Cabins were not pressurized, so airplanes had to fly around mountains. Flying at night was unsafe. Even in the late 1920s, travelers could cross the United States by train faster than by air (and much more comfortably to boot). In 1926, only 6,000 Americans traveled on commercial airliners.

While Boeing sold a number of planes to the military in the 1920s and early 1930s, sales of commercial planes were almost nonexistent until 1933, when the company started marketing its model 247. The twin-engine 247 was revolutionary and generally is recognized as the world's first modern airplane. It had a capacity to carry 10 passengers and a crew of 3. It had a cruising speed of 189 mph and could fly about 745 miles before needing to be refueled. It was the first plane used for regularly scheduled service between New York and the West Coast, a flight that took 20 hours, with seven stops. Seventy-five of the planes were sold before Boeing replaced the 247 with the much larger model 307 Stratoliner. The Stratoliner had a capacity of 33 passengers and a crew of 5. It could cruise at 220 mph and had a range of 2,390 miles. Importantly, the Stratoliner had a pressurized cabin, so it could fly above mountains and above turbulence. The Stratoliner should have been a winner, but the plane did not make its maiden flight until the last day of 1938, and World War II commenced before the plane became established. Only 10 were ever built.

Boeing helped the Allies defeat Germany. The Boeing B-17 Flying Fortress bomber and the B-29 Superfortress bomber became legendary. More than 12,500 B-17s and more than 3,500 B-29s were built (some by Boeing itself and some by other companies that had spare capacity). Boeing prospered during World War II, but at the end of the war, the Air Force immediately canceled orders for thousands of planes, and Boeing was forced to reduce its employment levels by 70,000 and redirect its efforts back to commercial aviation. The company then redesigned the B-29 into a four-engine, long-range commercial plane named the 377 Sratrocruiser, which first flew in mid-1947. However, the Stratocruiser soon was obsoleted by a destructive technology: the jet engine. In mid-1949, the de Havilland Aircraft Company started testing its Comet jetliner, and the Comet commenced carrying paying passengers three years later. It was clear that Boeing had to respond. And it did. Boeing started to develop its 707 jet in 1952. Tests started two years later and commercial flights in 1958. The 707 was a hit and soon became the leading commercial plane in the world.

Over the next 30 years, Boeing grew into a large and highly successful company. It introduced many models of popular commercial planes that covered a wide range of capacities, and it became a leader in the production of high-technology military aircraft and systems. Moreover, in 1996 and 1997, the company materially increased its size and capabilities by acquiring North American Aviation and McDonnell Douglas. Between 1960 and 2000, Boeing's revenues increased from $1.56 billion to $51.32 billion, and its net income increased from $25 million to $2,128 million.

In the 1990s, Boeing realized that it needed to find a replacement for its aging 767. Initially, the company considered two alternatives. The first was a plane that could travel just under the speed of sound and that had about the same fuel efficiency as the 767. The second was an enlarged version of the 747 that could compete head-on with Airbus's planned A-380. However, in 2002, Boeing dropped both alternatives in favor of a lightweight, carbon-composite, fuel-efficient aircraft that would offer about 20 percent reduced fuel consumption instead of higher speed or larger capacity. The proposed new model was named the 787 Dreamliner. Boeing completed the basic concept of the new plane by the end of 2003. Four months later, Japan's ANA became the 787's first customer, with an order of 50 planes. By the end of 2005, a total of 288 orders had been received. The large number of early orders verified the need for a new fuel-efficient plane.

The 787 required many new technologies. Strong and lightweight carbon fiber composites, which previously had not been used structurally on commercial aircraft, make up about 50 percent of the plane's primary structure, including its fuselage and wings. There are many other firsts. For example, each section of the fuselage is one piece of wrapped composite material. On previous Boeing planes, each section was made of about 1,500 sheets of aluminum held together by more than 40,000 fasteners.

Also, the 787 has new hydraulics, new engines, new landing gears, new electronic controls, new avionics, and new lithium-ion batteries. It is manufactured from 2.3 million parts. In spite of the newness and complexity, Boeing hoped to reduce the time to develop the plane from the normal six years to four years, with a first test flight scheduled for August 2007.

However, in January 2007, the 787 program started falling behind schedule. Suppliers were late delivering parts, some fasteners were improperly installed, segments of the wing needed to be redesigned, and some software was incomplete. Finally, on December 15, 2009, more than two years late, a 787 taxied down a runway in Everett, Washington, and lifted off for a three-hour maiden test flight. For the next nearly two years, Boeing extensively tested the 787 and found and corrected a number of "bugs." Many investors criticized Boeing for the bugs, but I was both sympathetic and understanding. To my way of thinking, it would be unreasonable to assume that Boeing could assemble 2.3 million parts into a newly designed plane without incurring some serious problems, especially since many of the structures and systems were new and advanced technologies.

On September 27, 2011, about three years late, ANA accepted delivery of its first 787. Thirty days later, after testing and training, the plane was placed in commercial service, carrying a full load of passengers from Tokyo to Hong Kong. ANA auctioned tickets for the inaugural commercial flight, with the highest bidder paying $34,000 for a seat.

But the 787 still experienced start-up problems. On February 6, 2012, Boeing said it discovered manufacturing errors in some fuselage sections. On July 23, 2012, defects were found in five Rolls-Royce engines. Five days later, a 787 engine failed during testing. On September 5, ANA was forced to abort a take-off after white smoke billowed from the left engine (the white smoke was caused by a breakdown in a hydraulic system). On December 5, the Federal Aviation Administration (FAA) ordered inspections of all 787s following reports of fuel leaks.

In late 2012, the media and Wall Street generally were highly critical of Boeing for the myriad of problems. After reading the criticism, I reasoned that the negativism likely was weighing on the price of Boeing's shares and that the price could appreciate materially once the start-up problems were solved. I decided to research and analyze the company.

I started with Boeing's balance sheet. I quickly noticed that the company had more cash than debt, even after investing more than $20 billion of cash in the development of the 787. However, the company did have large pension and health care liabilities: $23.0 billion versus only $8.2 billion five years earlier. I would need to analyze this $23.0 billion balance sheet liability before purchasing any shares, but first I would analyze the other key fundamentals of the company.

Boeing has two businesses: (1) commercial aviation and (2) defense. The production of larger commercial planes is a duopoly with almost impenetrable barriers to entry, as evidenced by the technology and pre-production costs required to produce the 787. Michael Porter, the highly respected professor at Harvard Business School, identifies five forces that should determine the long-term profitability of a company. Boeing's commercial aviation business passes Porter's five forces test with flying colors:

1. *Threat of new entrants.* It would require decades and tens of billions of dollars for a new entrant to develop and test planes that could compete with Boeing's and Airbus's larger planes. Furthermore, a new entrant would have to win the confidence of the airlines and the flying public.
2. *Threat of substitution.* I could not imagine that high-speed trains or ships, or any future new method of travel, would dent the demand for air travel in the immediate future.
3. *Power over suppliers.* Boeing is a very important customer for many of its suppliers, and Boeing has the option of playing one supplier off against another. It can tell a supplier that, unless it reduces price, it will lose future business to a competitor. Thus, Boeing has large bargaining power when negotiating price.
4. *Power of customers.* The airlines can and do seek bids from both Boeing and Airbus. However, some of Boeing's models sometimes are a better fit for a particular need. In particular, Boeing's

777 seems to have an edge over Airbus's long-distance wide-body planes. And, importantly, the 787, because of its fuel efficiency, has a competitive edge. In spite of all of the 787's problems and adverse publicity, by December 2012, Boeing had 799 orders for 787s valued at an estimated $100 billion. On balance, the commercial airplane business is competitive, but the competition is limited. Airplanes are far from being a commodity.

5. *Degree of rivalry.* Boeing and Airbus certainly were rivals, but both enjoyed large backlogs that should have mitigated cutthroat competition. In December 2012, Boeing had an undelivered firm backlog of about 4,300 airplanes, which, based on 2012 deliveries of 601 aircraft, equaled 7.1 years of production.

Boeing also seemed to have an experienced and talented management and an excellent reputation with the airlines and the flying public. Furthermore, because of the strong demand for new airplanes, Boeing's annual production was expected to increase from 601 planes in 2012 to more than 750 in 2015. The company's commercial business was booming.

Boeing's defense business, on the other hand, was not booming. The U.S. government was reining in its expenditures for defense. Some of the decline in demand was being offset by increased demand from foreign governments, but, on balance, it appeared likely that Boeing's defense revenues would decline slightly between 2012 and 2015. However, Boeing was reducing its costs to the extent that defense profits might be held flat, or even increase some.

Based on the preceding preliminary analysis, I made a model of Boeing's future earnings. The preliminary model concluded that the company could earn at least $7 per share in 2015. The shares at the time were selling at about $75, or at less than 11 times the $7—a very low price-to-earnings (PE) ratio for such a strong and well-positioned company. Thus, I was inspired to delve deeply into Boeing's fundamentals.

After a few weeks studying Boeing and thinking about the company's probable future, I decided to build a more detailed model of the company's earnings per share (EPS). The model would contain (1) estimates of 2015 earnings for each model of Boeing's commercial planes; (2) an estimate of 2015 earnings for the defense segment; (3) a projection of nonoperating expenses, including research, pension, and net interest; (4) the expected effective tax rate; and (5) the projected number of shares outstanding.

When calculating the profits of its commercial airplanes, Boeing uses "program" accounting. Under program accounting, Boeing first makes a conservative estimate of how many planes of a given model will be built. This quantity is known as the block size. Then, for the planes in the block, Boeing estimates the average price that will be received and the expected average cost per plane. Thus, the profitability of each plane in a block is relatively constant and predictable from year to year, except in years when there is a major revision in the block size or in the estimated average price or cost. I had reasonably good estimates of the profitability of each of Boeing's models, so, by knowing the projected production rate for each, I could estimate the 2015 profits for each model. I note that the 787 was expected to be only marginally profitable in 2015. My best information was that the average price of a 787 was roughly $125 million and that the average projected cash cost of producing the first 1,100 planes (which was the initial block size) was a bit over $100 million, indicating a cash profit of something under $25 million per plane. Boeing had capitalized more than $20 billion of the 787's design and preproduction costs—and this $20+ billion would be amortized over the 1,100 block size at a rate of about $20 million per plane. Thus, I guesstimated that, while the average cash profit per 787 in the block would be close to $25 million, the average reported profit would be only about $3 to $4 million. Boeing's 2015 production of 787s was expected to be 120 planes. Thus, in 2015, the operating profit of the 787s was estimated at only $360 to $480 million, or only $0.30 to $0.45 per share after taxes.

I then projected that the profits of Boeing's defense segment would remain relatively flat, that research and development expenses would decline some now that the 787 was in production, and that interest expense would remain flat.

The next step was to take a close look at pension expense. Boeing used generally accepted accounting principles (GAAP) for its earnings statements. Under GAAP accounting, when calculating pension liabilities and pension expense, future liabilities are discounted to reflect the value of time. The discount rate used is a function of longer-term interest rates on bonds. Between 2008 and 2012, longer-term interest rates fell by about 2.25 percent. This meant that Boeing's reported pension liabilities and reported pension expense increased sharply. I strongly believed that interest rates at the end of 2012 were abnormally and likely unsustainably low and, therefore, that Boeing's balance sheet overstated pension liabilities and that its income statement understated reported earnings. For each 1 percent future increase in interest rates, Boeing's pension liabilities and pension expense would decline by $9.1 billion and $930 million, respectively. Therefore, if interest rates returned to 2008 levels, Boeing's stated pension liabilities and pension expense would decline by about $20 billion and $2 billion, respectively. After reaching this conclusion, I no longer was concerned about the magnitude of the company's pension liabilities, and I was convinced that the company's reported earnings were understated because the true economic costs of funding the pension obligations were far less than the costs reported under GAAP. Many other companies were experiencing the same disparity in their pension accounting, and many had started to report non-GAAP earnings that adjusted pension expense to reflect economic costs. Would Boeing also start reporting non-GAAP earnings? I did not know, but I decided that my model should include two estimates for 2015 EPS, one based on GAAP and one based the economic costs of the pension plans.

After projecting Boeing's effective tax rate and diluted share count, I double-checked my model for reasonableness. Based on the assumptions in the model, which did seem reasonable, I concluded that Boeing's 2015 GAAP and non-GAAP earnings could be roughly $7.50 per share and $8.25 per share, respectively.

Next, I had to value the shares. In 2015, about two-thirds of the company's total estimated earnings would be from commercial aviation and the remaining one third from defense. I believed that Boeing's commercial aviation business was unusually attractive and was worth close to 20 times earnings (I settled on 19 times). The defense business could be divided into two subsegments: (1) sales to the U.S. government, which I believed was a subpar business, and (2) sales to foreign governments, which I believed was an above-average business. On balance, I valued the defense business at 15 times and, therefore, the whole company at about 17.7 times. I was convinced that the 17.7 PE ratio should be applied to projected non-GAAP earnings and, thus, that Boeing might be worth about $145 in 2015.

The $145 valuation appeared compelling versus the existing share price of about $75. However, before purchasing the shares, I had to consider the risks that the 787 program might develop unsolvable problems. The plane had been tested for nearly two years, had been approved by the FAA, and was in commercial service. Boeing's engineering-oriented management had a history of successfully solving technological problems. But what if the many problems that had recently plagued the airplane were more than just normal start-up problems and could not be solved, leading to large cancellations of orders? What if one or two planes crashed due to problems that previously had not been anticipated? Given everything I knew, the chances that the 787 program would have to be abandoned appeared tiny, but what would the consequences be? One consequence would be a very serious blow to Boeing's reputation. However, the cash charges of canceling the program likely would not be large relative to the strength of Boeing's balance sheet. And the 787 was projected to account for only about 18 percent of Boeing's revenues and 4 to 5 percent of its earnings in 2015. The price of Boeing's shares might fall sharply upon the announcement of a very serious 787 problem, but the company still would have estimated 2015 non-GAAP earnings in excess of $7.50 per share, and thus there appeared to be a large margin of safety for shareholders who paid about $75 for the shares.

In December 2012 and early January 2013, we established a large position in Boeing's shares. On January 7, at a time we were still purchasing shares, a battery caught fire in an empty 787 parked at Logan Airport.

Then, on January 16, an ANA-owned 787 made an emergency landing after one of its batteries caught fire. After the second fire, the FAA ordered the grounding of all 787s, and the price of Boeing's shares immediately fell by 3.4 percent to $74.34.

On Thursday, January 17, I received a telephone call from an investment manager. He was selling his holdings in Boeing because he was fearful that, if serious problems developed with the 787, his clients would criticize him for unwisely sticking with Boeing after there had been warning signs about the reliability of the plane. I tried to convince the manager that, even if the 787 did develop serious lasting problems, Boeing still had a thriving business producing other models, and therefore there was a large margin of safety in the shares. My analysis fell on deaf ears, and the other manager sold all his holdings. Most investment managers adopt two goals: (1) to earn a good return on their holdings and (2) to keep their clients happy. I have only one goal: to earn high returns. If I earn high returns (without taking large risks of permanent loss), then my clients likely will be happy. If a client is not happy because of any ill-determined reason, then I am happy if the client chooses to leave Greenhaven for another manager.

During February and March 2012, Boeing worked to enclose the lithium-ion batteries on the 787 so that any future fires could not damage parts of the plane exterior to the enclosures. This plan seemed to satisfy the FAA, and on April 19, the FAA lifted its grounding order. The price of Boeing's shares hit a nadir on January 29 at $73.65, remained in the mid-$70s during February, and then started appreciating in March, when it appeared that the battery problem would be solved. On April 19, the shares closed at $87.96. Six months later, the shares sold at $122.52. The investment manager who sold his shares in mid-January at about $75 made a large mistake. The way I look at it, in the investment business, there are risks in owning securities, but there also are risks in not owning securities that have favorable risk-to-reward profiles. The risks in not owning undervalued securities are the opportunity costs. An extreme example would be an investment manager who purchased only Treasury bills for his clients. After adjusting for taxes and inflation, clients who own only Treasury bills would, over time, experience large erosions in their real wealth. However, if the investment manager had purchased Boeing's shares for his clients, the clients would have earned large profits that would serve to protect their original capital against losses on any future unprofitable investments. If an investor turns a $75 initial investment into $122, then the investor could absorb $47 of future losses before being underwater on his original $75 investment. Sometimes the best defense is a sensible offense.

Boeing's shares continued to move higher in the fall of 2013 and finished the year at $136. By now, Wall Street generally believed that the 787 program would be successful and that Boeing would enjoy rising earnings and large cash flows that could be used to repurchase shares. We believed that a large percentage of the company's intermediate-term potential now had been discounted into the price of the shares, and we started to reduce the size of our holding.

I emphasize that I like to invest in strong and growing companies, such as Boeing, whose shares are temporarily depressed by understandable and solvable problems. However, I usually shy from investing in weak companies that are suffering from problems that stem from their weakness. Managements of weak companies often announce plans to improve earnings and other fundamentals, but my experience is that turning around entire companies usually is a difficult process that rarely meets with satisfactory success.

12

SOUTHWEST AIRLINES

August 2012. Josh was smiling broadly as he entered my office and said: "I have an idea that you will have a hard time liking. In fact, you will hate it. You might end up throwing me out of your office—forever. My idea is an airline. It is Southwest Airlines."

Josh was correct. I knew that the airlines were a terrible business. Among the worst. When an airplane flies from one city to another, the labor, fuel, and other costs of operating the plane are almost the same whether the plane is 100 percent filled with paying passengers, or 50 percent filled, or empty. Therefore, airlines have particularly large financial incentives to fill as many seats as possible. Because many passengers will choose a flight solely based on the price of the ticket, airlines historically try to fill seats by offering the lowest prices. The result has been severe price competition between airlines—in fact, destructive price competition. So destructive that the aggregate profits of the airline industry since the days of the Wright Brothers have been almost nonexistent.

Furthermore, the airline business is highly capital intensive because airplanes are expensive to purchase or lease. With low or no profits, most airlines have needed to borrow heavily to purchase aircraft, and thus most have balance sheets that are highly leveraged with debt or lease obligations.

During periods of weakness, many airlines have been unable to service their high debt loads or lease obligations and have been forced into bankruptcy, and many have simply disappeared, including Pan Am (1927–1991), TWA (1925–2001), Eastern (1926–1991), and Braniff (1928–1982). According to Wikipedia, between 1979 and 2011, fifty-two U.S. airlines filed for bankruptcy. Amazing! As Warren Buffett wrote in his 2007 annual report to Berkshire Hathaway shareholders: "Indeed, if a farsighted capitalist had been present at Kitty Hawk, he would have done his successors a huge favor by shooting Orville down."

The years 2001 through 2011 were particularly miserable for the airline industry. The sharp drop in travel after 9/11 was followed by a sharp increase in fuel costs and then by another sharp drop in travel during the 2008–2010 recession. Most of the large U.S. airlines incurred sizable losses in the 2000s and struggled to survive. United Airlines declared bankruptcy in 2002, Delta and Northwest in 2005, American in 2011.

Josh believed that the miserable conditions in the 2000s would trigger a period of prosperity for the airlines. Here's why. Airlines suffering large losses do not have the financial incentives or financial wherewithal to purchase many new airplanes. If fact, they have incentives to reduce costs by selling their less efficient planes. And that is exactly what happened between the years 2000 and 2011, with the result that the effective capacity of the domestic airlines declined by 3.1 percent from 701.5 billion seat-miles to 679.5 billion seat-miles. And during the same 11-year period that capacity declined by 3.1 percent, the demand for domestic air travel, largely driven by population growth, increased by 12.4 percent from 502.3 billion seat-miles to 564.7 billion. As a result, whereas the average flight in 2000 operated at 71.6 percent capacity, the average flight in 2011 operated at 83.1 percent of capacity.

Because most flights that depart at unpopular hours or that fly to less popular locations do so with many empty seats, if the entire airline industry operates at 83.1 percent of capacity, then many of the more popular flights will operate at full capacity—and many with wait lists.

Josh's thesis was that capacity would continue to tighten because relatively few new airplanes were on order by the domestic carriers. He believed that, as capacity tightened further, the domestic carriers would be able to increase their prices and that the increased prices would lead to much higher profits and much higher share prices for the airlines.

At the time Josh entered my office, Southwest Airlines' shares were selling at only a touch above their book value of $8.34. Unlike almost any other domestic airline, Southwest had been continuously profitable for decades and had as much cash as debt. The company had earned an excellent reputation as a well-managed and highly reliable low-cost carrier. Amazingly, Southwest was the fourth most admired company in the whole world, according to *Fortune* magazine's 2011 survey. Southwest was ahead of Procter & Gamble (the fifth most admired company), Coca-Cola (#6), Amazon (#7), FedEx (#8), and Microsoft (#9). The only other airline that made Fortune's top 50 list was Singapore Airlines at #18.

Southwest Airlines was incorporated by Herb Kelleher and Rollin King on March 15, 1967, as Air Southwest Company. The initial plan was to fly only between three major cities in Texas: Dallas, Houston, and San Antonio. Kelleher, who was the leader of the two founders, believed that by being an intrastate carrier within Texas, Air Southwest could avoid burdensome federal regulations. However, litigation delayed the start-up of the new airline when Braniff, Continental Airlines, and Trans-Texas sued to block the addition of a new competitor. The suit labored in the Texas courts for more than two years, but in late 1970, the Texas Supreme Court upheld Air Southwest's rights to form a regional airline. In March 1971, Air Southwest changed its name to Southwest Airlines, and three months later the brand new airline commenced service between Dallas, Houston, and San Antonio with three (soon four) Boeing 737s.

From inception, Herb Kelleher decided to model Southwest after Pacific Southwest Airlines, a California-based regional carrier that was founded in 1949. Pacific Southwest was the first major carrier to offer discount fares. In addition, it attempted to attract customers by making flying fun. Flight attendants and pilots were encouraged to joke with passengers. In the 1960s, the flight attendants' uniforms included miniskirts—and in the 1970s, when fashions changed, hot pants. The company painted a smile on the nose of each of its planes. Keeping with the desired ethos of the company, Pacific Southwest's founder, Ken Friedkin, wore brightly colored Hawaiian shirts. Pacific Southwest's slogan was "The World's Friendliest Airline," and the friendliness worked and attracted paying customers.

While potential competitors normally are not friendly to each other, Ken Friedkin seemed flattered that Herb Kelleher was interested in copying Pacific Southwest's business model and generously agreed to help train some of Southwest's repair mechanics and to offer Southwest flight, operating, and training manuals.

Kelleher selected Love Field in Dallas for the company's headquarters and adopted the word "love" as the company's motto for early advertisements. Beverages served to passengers were known as "love potions" and peanuts as "love bites." The company stock ticker symbol on the New York Stock Exchange was LUV. A committee formed to select flight attendants included an individual who had selected the attendants for Hugh Hefner's Playboy airplane. The flight attendants selected by the committee were described as cheerleaders, majorettes, or long-legged dancers with outgoing personalities. Herb Kelleher dressed them in hot pants and go-go boots. Clearly, Southwest was closely following Pacific Southwest's offbeat, fun, and successful model.

It is difficult to start up a new airline. Passengers usually feel safer flying with an established carrier that has a track record for reliability and safety. Southwest had difficulty attracting passengers in 1971 and 1972 and was unprofitable—so unprofitable that the company had to sell one of its four 737s to meet its payroll and other expenses. To compensate for the loss of 25 percent of its capacity, Southwest found ways to substantially reduce the time each remaining airplane remained on the ground between flights. This was the start of a concerted effort by Kelleher to model Southwest into a highly efficient, very low-cost carrier.

With low costs, low ticket prices, and a "love" business model, Southwest started to become successful by the mid-1970s. Its revenues in 1975 grew to $23 million, up from $15 million in 1974 and $9 million in 1973. The company about broke even in 1973, was in the black in 1974, and earned $3.4 million after taxes in 1975. The profitability permitted Southwest to purchase additional aircraft. By 1978, the company operated 13 Boeing 737s that serviced 11 Texas cities. Revenues and after-tax profits in 1978 were $81 and $17 million. Southwest Airlines was on the map.

In 1978, the airline industry became largely deregulated, and Southwest decided to expand outside of Texas. Its first interstate flight was from Houston to New Orleans on January 25, 1979. During the next two years, buoyed by the success of its low-cost, low-fare strategy, Southwest continued gradually to expand its service to additional cities. By 1980, the company was servicing 14 cities. Its revenues and after-tax profits in 1980 increased to $213 million and $29 million. In its 1980 annual report, management stated that the company's "unique combination of low fares, frequent service on short-haul routes, exemplary employee productivity, and high utilization of its assets" had saved its passengers substantial sums of money and, at the same time, had "achieved the highest operating profit margin of any domestic air carrier and had achieved, over the past five years, an annual return on stockholder equity of 37%."

During the next 20 years, Southwest continued to grow rapidly, partially due to the expansion of its network to most major cities in the United States, partially due to its low costs and fares, and partially due to its innovation and good management. Between 1980 and 2000, the company's revenues increased at a 16.6 percent compound annual growth rate (CAGR) from $213 million to $4,628 million, and its net earnings increased at a 16.5 percent CAGR from $28.4 million to $603.1 million. To remain low cost during the two decades, Southwest stressed simplicity. To reduce maintenance and training costs, it owned and flew only one model of aircraft: Boeing 737s. To avoid congestion, it used smaller airports, in Dallas preferring Love Field to DFW and in Chicago preferring Midway to O'Hare. To save booking costs, Southwest was one of the first airlines to sell tickets over the Internet and to issue ticketless tickets. Also, passengers were not able to reserve assigned seats, but instead selected their own seats on a first-come, first-serve basis upon boarding an aircraft. To further reduce costs, the company built its own computerized reservation system. If you are in a commodity business, the winners are those with the lowest costs—and Southwest had very low costs and was a winner.

The following story is instructive of Herb Kelleher's inventiveness and style. In March 1992, shortly after Southwest started using the motto "Just Plane Smart," Stevens Aviation Inc., a company that maintained aircraft and that had been using the "Just Plane Smart" motto for a number of years, threatened to sue Southwest for violating its trademark. After some discussions, instead of a lawsuit, Herb Kelleher and Stevens's CEO Kurt Herwald decided to settle the argument though an arm-wrestling match at the Dallas Sportatorium wrestling arena. A promotional video was created that showed the CEO's "training" for the match. In the video, Herb Kelleher is shown being aided by an assistant as he attempts a sit-up. A bottle of Wild Turkey whiskey waits as a reward for each completed sit-up. There were three rounds to the arm-wrestling match. The loser of each round had to pay $5,000 to a charity of his choice. The winner of two out of the three rounds gained use of the "Just Plane Smart" trademark. Kurt Herwald won two out of the three rounds, but he immediately granted co-use of "Just Plane Smart" to Southwest. The result of the arm-wrestling match was that both companies could use the trademark, charities received $15,000, and both companies received excellent publicity.

By 2011, Southwest's revenues had increased to more than $15 billion, but during the 2001–2011 period, the carrier's earnings per share (EPS) declined from a peak of $0.79 in 2000 to only $0.40 in 2011. Increased fuel costs and the soft economy were the causes of the sharp decline in earnings.

In August 2012, when Josh entered my office, Wall Street generally was unenthusiastic about the outlook for Southwest, and no Wall Street analyst was predicting a several-fold increase in EPS due to improved pricing. On July 19, the day after Southwest announced its results for the June quarter, several analysts issued reports on the company. The shares were trading at about $9.15 at the time. Goldman Sachs predicted that the company's

EPS would increase to $0.99 in 2014 and valued the shares at $8.50. Merrill Lynch projected that EPS would increase to $1.20 in 2014 and valued the shares at $9.50. Barclays was more optimistic. It projected that EPS would increase to $1.35 in 2014 and that the shares were worth $14. Josh, however, believed that if his thesis on pricing proved correct, earnings could soar far above Wall Street's estimates. His logic was as follows. The company's revenues in 2012 were expected to be about $16 billion. For every 1 percent increase in ticket prices, Southwest's pretax earnings would increase by $160 million and its net earnings would increase by about $0.13 per share, assuming an effective tax rate of 39 percent and a diluted share count of 745 million. Josh believed that as the demand for domestic air travel continued to approach capacity, ticket prices could increase by at least 4 to 5 percent per year, or 2 to 3 percent above assumed cost increases of about 2 percent of revenues. If real prices increased by 2 to 3 percent per year for four years, then the price increases would add $1.04 to $1.56 to EPS by 2016. Furthermore, Southwest recently had announced a profit improvement program that was projected to increase annual pretax earnings by $1,100 million by the end of 2015. The $1,100 million was composed of three pieces:

1. The company had just acquired AirTrans, another regional carrier. The annual synergistic savings of integrating AirTrans into Southwest were estimated at $400 million.
2. In addition, AirTrans flew a number of inefficient Boeing 717s. Transitioning the 717s to another carrier would save about $200 million per year.
3. Finally, Southwest had found a way to add an additional row of six seats to its 737-800s. The extra row of seats, a new reservations system, and other operational improvements together were expected to add about $500 million to annual pretax profits.

The $1,100 million profit program, if successful, would add about $0.90 to earnings by 2016. Based on these estimates and assumptions,

Josh concluded that there was a reasonable possibility that Southwest's EPS could increase from about $0.60 in 2012 to more than $2 in 2015 and to more than $2.50 in 2016, before other considerations. And there were two other considerations. The first was normal demand growth over the next several years. The second was that Southwest, which had as much cash as debt and which was generating large amounts of excess cash, had established an aggressive share repurchase plan. Josh estimated that the repurchase plan could reduce the diluted number of shares outstanding from 774 million in 2011 to materially below 700 million in 2016. Josh commented that the growth in demand and the share repurchase plan were icing on an already delicious cake, and they gave him some extra confidence that if prices increased by 4 to 5 percent per year, Southwest's EPS could exceed $2.50 in 2016.

Josh then used a second methodology to check the reasonableness of his projections. He estimated that Southwest's revenues would grow to about $19.5 billion by 2016. During the three years before the 9/11 terrorist attacks, Southwest's operating profit margins ranged between 16.4 percent and 18.1 percent. Josh reasoned that if he were correct that industry conditions would turn strong, Southwest's profit margins could return to the 16 to 18 percent level, and thus its operating profits in 2016 could be in the range of $3,200 to $3,500 million. After subtracting $125 million of interest expense from the $3,200 to $3,500 million of operating profits, after deducting taxes at a 39 percent effective rate, and based on an estimated diluted share count of 675 million, Josh's second methodology concluded that Southwest's estimated EPS in 2016 would be $2.75 to $3.

Josh also mentioned that he briefly analyzed the fundamentals of the three other large U.S. domiciled airlines, and while each also would materially benefit from increased pricing, each had a precarious balance sheet. For example, on June 30, 2012, Delta had $8.8 billion of net debt and a tangible book value of negative $11.0 billion. United had $4.3 billion of net debt and a tangible book value of negative $3.3 billion. American was in bankruptcy. Southwest, by comparison, had no net debt and had a tangible book value of a positive $5.9 billion. Josh believed that if the airline industry hit an unexpected bump, such as a spike in fuel prices, a terrorist attack, or a sharp recession, the airlines with the precarious balance sheets might be forced into real or quasi bankruptcy, with the result that their shareholders might suffer material permanent losses. Josh believed that Delta's and United's shares possibly had even more upside potential than Southwest's, but they were not for us. Greenhaven hates permanent loss.

Josh attempted to value Southwest's shares. What was the value of a gem of a company in a miserable feast-or-famine business? Josh did not have the foggiest idea. Neither did I. We did not have a reasonable approach to valuing the shares. However, we did not need to. If Southwest earned anything close to $2.50 per share in 2016, the shares likely would appreciate sharply—possibly several-fold from the present price of about $9. And, equally important, the company's quality and balance sheet would provide considerable protection against permanent loss. We thought we had a winner—a possible home run.

Josh set up a telephone call with Tammy Romo, Southwest's chief financial officer. We peppered Tammy with questions, trying to find a hole in our analysis. We did not find a hole. In fact, the more we learned and thought about Southwest, the more we concluded that its reward-to-risk ratio was particularly favorable—in fact, compelling.

So, I did not throw Josh out of my office, but instead soon started purchasing Southwest's shares. If you had asked me a year earlier whether Greenhaven ever was likely to own shares of an airline, I would have said, "No way." But I believe that investors sometimes need to be open to new ideas that challenge previous convictions. In the investment business, as in life, one becomes disadvantaged if one develops tunnel vision.

Soon after we established a position in Southwest, I told my 15-year-old grandson Grant about the purchase. Grant was 6 feet 1 inch tall and had the frame of a football player, which he was. Grant had an immediate adverse reaction to Southwest: "Eddie (all my grandchildren call me by my nickname), Southwest's seats are cramped, and you must arrive at the gate at least an hour early to get a decent seat; I call the airline *Southworst*." Well, most passengers are not football players and, unlike Grant, most have to pay their own fares and therefore appreciate the airline's low discount prices, even if they cannot reserve a seat ahead of time.

The price of Southwest's shares started appreciating sharply soon after we started establishing our position. Sometimes it takes years before one of our holdings starts to appreciate sharply—and sometimes we are lucky with our timing. In the case of Southwest, we were lucky. The stock market turned strong in early 2013, and some investors became optimistic about the intermediate-term outlook for the airline industry. Most of the Wall Street firms, however, still were not projecting that the airlines would be able to sharply increase their prices and earnings. For example, between the fall of 2012 and the spring of 2013, Goldman Sachs's analysts slightly decreased their 2014 EPS estimate for Southwest from $0.99 to $0.95. On October 7, 2013, while Goldman's analysts wrote that they were encouraged by Southwest's present pricing discipline, they increased their 2014 EPS estimate by only a few cents to $0.98. Then, on October 24, Southwest announced that the company had earned $0.34 per share in the third quarter of 2013, up 161 percent from $0.13 in the comparable 2012 quarter. Virtually all of the large increase in EPS was due to price increases. According to our calculations, prices per revenue passenger mile increased by 8.6 percent if one adjusts for changes in the price of jet fuel. On the day of the earnings release, Goldman finally started to get the message and increased its 2014 EPS to $1.12. The price of Southwest's shares rose 3.7 percent on the day of the release, and the shares now were selling at about twice the price they were selling at on the day Josh first walked into my office with a broad smile and the idea. Goldman and most other Wall Street firms had failed to predict that ticket prices would increase sharply due to a tightening market. In my opinion, Goldman's analysts had been so focused on Southwest's recent developments that they had failed to step back and correctly analyze and predict the critical fundamentals that would determine the intermediate-term price of Southwest's shares. They had become reporters of recent news, not analysts.

On with the story. In the fourth quarter of 2013, Southwest's ticket prices increased by 6.4 percent (again, adjusted for the price of jet fuel), and ticket prices continued to increase at favorable rates in early 2014. By the spring of 2014, Wall Street generally had become more aware of the new momentum in prices and profitability. Common EPS estimates for 2014 had increased to about $1.50, but most firms still were projecting only modest EPS gains after 2014. Goldman Sachs, for example, was projecting $1.50 for 2014, $1.72 for 2015, and $1.86 for 2016. Josh believed that if $1.50 was the correct estimate for 2014, then normal annual growth, plus the $1,100 million profit improvement, plus share repurchases would result in 2016 EPS far above Goldman's $1.86 before any additional price increases—and he thought it logical that the domestic airlines would continue to increase ticket prices as the market continued to tighten.

In late spring, Josh, Chris, and I spent considerable time thinking about our investment in Southwest. At the time, the shares were selling at $25 to $26. We tried to estimate what the shares would be worth in a year or two, but we ended up being befuddled. We had no methodology to estimate what the company's earnings would be in a normal environment. The airline business had been a feast-or-famine (and mostly famine) business, and there had been almost no periods of normalcy. Moreover, while we had methodologies to value excellent companies in excellent businesses and excellent companies in mediocre businesses, we did not have an approach to value an excellent company in an absolutely miserable business.

Finally, we decided to sell about half of our holdings in Southwest. The shares had appreciated by far more than our other holdings, and thus they had become too large a percentage of our portfolios given the normal unattractiveness of the airline business. And with the price of the shares up nearly threefold from the day Josh first adopted his thesis, their risk-to-reward ratio was not nearly as favorable as it had been. Often, when I am in a quandary about whether to sell one of our holdings, I sell half or some other fraction that makes sense under the circumstances.

The price of Southwest's shares continued to appreciate during the summer of 2014, reaching close to $35 early in the fall. The company was doing better than we had expected. Demand was strong. Capacity was tight. Prices were firm and increasing. The cost of jet fuel was declining some. We knew all this, but so did other investors. The good news was out, the shares no longer had a favorable risk-to-reward ratio, and we decided to sell the remainder of our holding.

13

GOLDMAN SACHS

During the spring of 2014, I spent hundreds of hours looking for new investment ideas. I screened lists of stocks, thought about various industries that might be attractive, read magazines and newspapers, brainstormed with my associates, and reviewed lists of stocks recently purchased by other investment managers.[1] But frustration was my companion. I could not find an attractive idea. I looked and looked and looked, but to no avail.

Then, on Friday, May 30, I noticed that the cover and lead story in the latest edition of *Bloomberg* magazine was about the three co-heads of Goldman Sachs's investment banking business: David Solomon, Richard Gnodde, and John S. Weinberg. I had worked with John Weinberg's grandfather, Sidney Weinberg, in 1966 and 1967, and had known John S.'s father, John L. Weinberg, who had been the co–senior partner of Goldman Sachs for many years. I decided to read the story, largely for entertainment. The article emphasized the strength and profitability of Goldman's investment banking operations.

Out of curiosity, I went to my Bloomberg terminal and looked up Goldman's share price: $159.80. I then looked up the company's tangible book value[2] per share: $145.04. Flash through the mind! Goldman was a premier company that was selling at only a 10 percent premium to its tangible book value. Second flash through the mind! Goldman had two businesses that required very little capital (investment banking and investment management) and two businesses that required considerable capital ("trading" and investing). By calculating what the non-capital-intensive businesses should earn in a normal environment and by estimating that the capital-intensive businesses should be earning more than a 10 percent return on equity,[3] I could estimate Goldman's earnings power. Thus, I had an approach to modeling the company's earnings.

I downloaded the company's recent income statements. The non-capital-intensive businesses were earning $5+ per share after taxes in what appeared to be a somewhat subnormal environment for the businesses. I estimated that $4 of Goldman's book value should be allocated to the non-capital-intensive activities and therefore that the remaining $141 per share should be allocated to trading and investing. Thus, I concluded that the earnings power of trading and investing should be more than $14 per share and that the earnings power of the whole company should be about $20 per share, which works out to approximately a 14 percent return on tangible book value. When I project estimates and returns, I think about the reasonableness of the estimates. Do they seem realistic? In this case, my conclusion that Goldman's earnings power should be about 14 percent of its tangible book value made a great deal of sense to me. Much of investing is about reasonability, common sense, and judgment.

When valuing companies, we usually look out two years to the future. If Goldman's earnings power was about $20 now, its earnings power certainly should be at least $22 by 2016 (the financial markets tend to grow at a 5 to 6 percent annual rate). I then thought about a deserved price-to-earnings (PE) ratio. The non-capital-intensive businesses were gems that should be worth a higher-than-average PE ratio. However, trading and investing were less attractive business lines that likely were worth less than an average PE ratio. On balance, I decided to value Goldman's shares at 12 to 15 times their earnings power. Therefore, an early and preliminary conclusion was that Goldman's shares could be worth $265 to $330 by 2016, or 65 to 105 percent above their present price. I finally had a possible idea.

I was excited. I dropped everything else I was doing and started reading Goldman's Form 10-K. I particularly was looking for information that was counter to my initial analysis that the company's shares were materially undervalued. I spent considerable time reading about pending litigation, which mainly stemmed from alleged unethical trades and other actions made prior to the 2008–2009 financial crisis. We generally shy away from investing in companies whose ethical standards are questionable, but I was convinced that the ethical lapses at Goldman were the doings of a relatively small percentage of the company's 32,000 employees—and that the firm itself should not be faulted for the mal-advice given and the mal-transactions enacted by a relatively small number of its employees. It would be unreasonable to assume that any firm could hire 32,000 employees that did not include some bad actors. In my opinion, one should be careful not to condemn an entire organization for the immoral or illegal actions of a few.

Next, I studied Goldman's balance sheet. After the financial crisis, the company decided to materially deleverage itself. In 2007, Goldman's assets were 26 times as large as its shareholders' equity. By the end of 2013, the ratio had declined to less than 12 times. I then tried to analyze the quality of the balance sheet, but this was difficult to do, partially because the assets owned by Goldman can change day to day. However, I did feel comfortable knowing that, as a result of the 2008 financial crisis, Goldman's financial strength continually was being scrutinized by many regulatory bodies. Also, the Federal Reserve Bank had permitted Goldman to reacquire $6.2 billion of its shares in 2013, after reacquiring $4.6 billion in 2012 and $6.0 billion 2011. I believed that the Fed would not have permitted these large repurchases if the governors and their staff did not feel highly confident about the strength of Goldman's balance sheet. The Fed can make a mistake. No business decision can be based on assuredly accurate information—and situations can change. But in an imperfect world, the scrutiny of the Fed still was an important consideration when analyzing the risks of owning Goldman's shares.

Furthermore, while I always have been concerned about asset quality after a long period of prosperity because continuing prosperity often breeds overconfidence and resulting misassessments of risks, the reverse also should be true. After a scary financial crisis and a deep recession, managements usually are prone to be particularly risk averse.

A large segment of Goldman's 10-K dealt with the increased regulation on investment banks. Many on Wall Street viewed the increased regulation as a negative. But I also saw it as a silver lining. The sharply increased capital requirements likely would cause weaker and less profitable firms to withdraw from some lines of business, thus reducing competition. Also, the costs of complying with Dodd-Frank and the other regulations would serve as large barriers to entry for possible new competitors. Thus, an unintended consequence of Dodd-Frank was to stifle competition and to increase the power and market shares of the large, well-capitalized financial institutions.

After reading the 10-K, I immediately convened a meeting with Greenhaven's two other analysts: my son, Chris, and Josh Sandbulte. The three of us spent the next two hours discussing the pros and cons of Goldman Sachs's businesses. We brainstormed. Our conclusions were that Goldman was a very strong company in a reasonably attractive industry and that the company's shares were trading at a deeply undervalued and undeserved level. We reasoned that the shares were depressed because many investors generally remained concerned about the balance sheet risks of financial service companies and because many were concerned that the industry would become overregulated. We believed that these concerns were overblown and would mitigate with time. They were our opportunity.

I was amused that Goldman Sachs earned $15.46 per share in 2013, up sharply from $5.87 per share 10 years earlier. During the 10-year period, the company had suffered through the worst financial crisis and the worst recession since the Great Depression and through hostile litigation and hostile legislation, and yet the company's profits had increased by 163 percent. My experience is that analysts and historians often dwell too much on a company's recent problems and underplay its strengths, progress, and promise. An analogy might be the progress of the United States during the twentieth century. At the end of the century, U.S. citizens generally were far wealthier, healthier, safer, and better educated than at the start of the century. In fact, the century was one of extraordinary progress. Yet most history books tend to mainly focus on the two tragic world wars, the highly unpopular Vietnam War, the Great Depression, the civil unrest during the Civil Rights movement, and the often poor leadership in Washington. The century was littered with severe problems and mistakes. If you only had read the newspapers and the history books, you likely would have concluded that the United States had suffered a century of relative and absolute decline. But the United States actually exited the century strong and prosperous. So also did Goldman exit 2013 strong and prosperous.

Bloomberg archives many presentations made by managements. I wanted to hear what Goldman's management was saying publicly, so I listened to about 10 recent presentations. I was particularly intrigued by comments made on May 30, 2013, by Gary Cohn, Goldman's president and chief operating officer. Cohn stated that, in spite of a challenging environment in 2012, Goldman had been able to earn a 10.7 percent return on its equity (ROE). He added: "We are focused on positioning the firm to further expand our ROE … as the operating environment improves." He elaborated on "opportunities we see to drive returns higher over the medium term." One driver was revenues. Cohn pointed out that investment banking revenues had been cyclically low in recent years—and a return to normal activities would give revenues and earnings a major boost. He added that Goldman also had the opportunity to gain market share in investment banking because a number of competitors were retrenching in the wake of the financial crisis and in reaction to resulting increased regulation and higher capital requirements. Cohn emphasized: "You do not need a significant amount of retrenchment to create an important revenue opportunity for us."

Cohn also emphasized that Goldman's cost reductions should add to earnings. He stated that the company recently had completed a $1.9 billion cost reduction program and that the firm's compensation expense as a percentage of revenues had materially declined over the past few years.

Gary Cohn made another point that sparked my imagination. He stated that Goldman "will continue to adjust and reallocate resources to maximize efficiency as necessary; we have a culture of adaptability." My thought was that, if one area of Goldman's activities was producing subnormal returns, the company could remove capital from that area in favor of another area that was producing high returns. This flexibility is a positive attribute of many financial service companies. Manufacturing companies, however, often are saddled with poorly designed or poorly located plants. If labor costs in Brazil become materially lower than labor costs in Alabama, it would be nearly impossible for a paper company to pick up a paper mill located in Alabama and ship it to Brazil.

Goldman's presentations generally exuded a calm confidence in the company's future. Their content signaled that management was aggressive and ambitious, but not arrogant. I realized that the presentations were carefully scripted, but nonetheless I was favorably impressed.

I then telephoned three acquaintances who had been high-level executives at Goldman. Each had similar impressions: management was excellent; the younger employees tended to be among the best and the brightest; bright and ambitious employees will find ways to make money for themselves and for the firm; and the firm continued to enjoy the best brand image in the business.

Experience builds intuition, and my intuition was to start purchasing shares in Goldman. The concept, the fundamentals, and the profit potential seemed compelling. Mr. Arthur Ross frequently counseled me that "we are not a debating society; we are not a debating society; act, Ed, act." So I acted—and placed an order to buy shares of Goldman Sachs. Within a few weeks, we purchased a full position in the shares.

About a month later, I had lunch with Will Gordon, an investment manager at a medium-sized firm. I told Will that our Goldman idea was a godsend because we were having difficulty finding new ideas post the strong stock market in 2013. I also mentioned that our portfolios had appreciated substantially more than the market in 2013 and that we now had more than $5 billion under management and needed to find stocks that we could purchase in size, such as Goldman. I added that, given the level of the stock market and given our increased size, it was a challenge to keep our portfolios appreciating at buoyant rates. Will's immediate comment was, "Well, Ed, I guess you will have to settle for lower returns in the future." I had an immediate immensely adverse reaction to Will's comment—and especially to the use of the word *settle*. Settle was not part of my investing vocabulary and would not be in the future. All my life I enjoyed the thrill of competing to win. I would not "settle" to play mediocre tennis, to have a mediocre round of golf, nor to have mediocre investment results. As a senior at Williams College, every day I walked past Hopkins Gate. Chiseled on one stone pillar of the Gate was the motto:

> *Climb high, climb far,*
> *Your goal the sky,*
> *Your aim the star*

That is my mantra. I aspire to build a ladder to the stars and climb on every single rung. I believe that ambition, tempered by reason, permits a person to succeed and feel rewarded, and that, in a competitive world, settling for mediocrity often leads to failure. Yes, investing $5 billion at a time when the stock market is relatively fully valued is a challenge. But there are two disparate mind-sets to the word *challenge*. One is the frustration of encountering an apparently impenetrable wall. The other is the thrill and satisfaction of climbing the wall. To each his own, but I relish the latter. And I say hogwash to "settling" for lower returns in the future.

On a bright day in the fall of 2014, I received an invitation to have a breakfast meeting with Abebayo ("Bayo") Ogunlesi, the lead director of Goldman's board of directors. The main purpose of the breakfast was to discuss the company's governance. I readily accepted the invitation. On the appointed day, I arrived at Goldman's West Street headquarters about 45 minutes early. I believe that it is rude to be late to meetings, so I normally allow too much time for travel, fearing that a train will be late or that I will have difficulty hailing a cab. It is a Wachenheim idiosyncrasy. One of many. Usually when I am early, I kill time with a cup of coffee or a walk around the neighborhood. However, on this occasion, I made good use of the 45 spare minutes. I took an express elevator to Goldman's 11th floor, which serves as a sky lobby. Most of Goldman's employees change elevators on the 11th floor, and many come to grab a cup of coffee or a snack at the floor's cafeteria. I found a comfortable chair, and for a good part of the 45 minutes, I people watched. By studying how Goldman's employees communicate with each other, dress, and walk, I could get some sense of the type of people who work for the company. And I was impressed. The employees generally were friendly toward each other, smiley, neatly dressed, and seemingly intent upon their purpose. And I was impressed by the 11th floor itself, which was functionally laid out, elegant, in good taste, and definitely not gold plated. While it is dangerous to judge a book by its cover, I do find it useful to observe a company's employees and offices.

A few minutes before the scheduled 9:00 a.m. breakfast meeting with Bayo Ogunlesi, I took an elevator to one of the top floors of the headquarters building and was escorted to Goldman's boardroom. Just inside the boardroom, a spread of bagels, fruits, orange juice, and coffee was laid out on a cart. No eggs any way you like them. No bacon. No pancakes or French toast. And no waiters dressed in tuxedos. Just a simple, self-service breakfast. My favorable impression of Goldman Sachs increased by another notch. Goldman was not trying to impress its guests with opulence.

Bayo's background is amazing. Born in the small rural village of Makun, Nigeria, he attended high school at Kings College in Lagos and then left Nigeria to attend Oxford. After receiving a BA at Oxford, he attended both Harvard Business School and Harvard Law School at the same time and, along with a classmate, became one of the first two students of African descent to become an editor of the *Harvard Law Review.* After receiving his LLB in 1979, Bayo clerked for Thurgood Marshall, becoming the first non-American ever to clerk at the U.S. Supreme Court. In 1983, Bayo joined Cravath, Swaine & Moore in New York City, but after several months practicing law, Credit Suisse asked Cravath if they could borrow Bayo to help negotiate and finance a $6 billion liquefied natural gas plant in Nigeria. Bayo never returned to Cravath, but instead quickly rose through the ranks of Credit Suisse, eventually heading the firm's global banking division and being elected to the firm's board of directors. In 2006, Bayo left Credit Suisse to become a cofounder of a private equity firm, Global Infrastructure Partners, which makes infrastructure investments, especially in the energy, transportation, and water industries. Who says that America is not a land of opportunity.

During the taxi ride to Goldman's headquarters, I thought about the upcoming meeting and predicted that Bayo would emphasize that Goldman's board is quite independent from management, that the board focuses on controlling risks, and that the board would keep a lid on management's compensation. These were three obvious key issues. Sure enough, Bayo focused on the three issues, giving sales pitches that were designed to comfort a shareholder. Thus, I did not learn much from the meeting, but I had not expected to.

Another consideration weighed on my mind. Bayo was affable, articulate, and seemingly knowledgeable about Goldman Sachs's operations. But how much could he really know? He had a full-time job elsewhere. His knowledge of Goldman probably mainly came from what management told him and from information in materials prepared for board meetings. Directors are outsiders. They normally cannot unobtrusively wander around the offices and trading desks of Goldman to find out what really is going on. I will never forget a board meeting of the lead smelting company that I was a director of in the 1970s. The meeting was held at a secondary smelter. At secondary smelters, old car batteries are crushed and processed to separate the lead from other materials. The lead is then purified in a furnace and resold. Secondary smelters tend to be dirty—in fact, filthy. When a battery is being crushed, it is difficult to contain all the lead and other materials in a controlled space. Yet the smelter where the board meeting was held was spotless. I imagined that the workers at the smelter spent hours with brushes, vacuum cleaners, mops, towels, chemicals, and even toothbrushes cleansing the smelter in advance of the arrival of the directors. My suspicions were corroborated when I took a bathroom break during the meeting. In the men's room, after drying my hands, I noticed that the towel disposal container was filled with about 50 empty cans of Pledge. Similarly, I believe that the information that directors receive about a company usually is carefully scrubbed by management, who continually wish to look as good as possible.

In mid-December, I received an e-mail from Bayo announcing the election of two new directors to Goldman's board. The e-mail included resumes. I was impressed, not only by the quality of the new directors, but especially by the effort Bayo made to e-mail me (and likely other larger shareholders as well) about the election. The e-mail reminded me of a comment made more than 40 years earlier by Bob Menschel, a friend, who by coincidence was a top executive at Goldman Sachs at the time. Bob's comment was that small caring efforts toward employees pay off in favorable relationships and favorable morale. Remember birthdays. Ask about children or vacation plans. Occasionally, take an employee out to lunch. Buy employees small Christmas presents. Bayo was following Bob's advice, and it paid off. Somebody at Goldman (Bayo or a person on his staff) made the effort to care about Greenhaven and me, and my positive feelings toward Goldman increased by yet another notch.

In May 2015, I received another invitation to Goldman's headquarters, this time to meet with Gary Cohn and CFO Harvey Schwartz. Again, I leapt at the opportunity. The previous month, Goldman had reported that it had earned a surprisingly strong $5.94 per share in the first quarter of 2015, which was equal to a 15 percent return on tangible equity. The $5.94 is, of course, equivalent to an annualized earnings rate of nearly $24 per share. Remember, I had been projecting that Goldman might earn about $22 per share in 2016. Therefore, at least in the first quarter of 2015, Goldman's earnings already were exceeding my projections.

At the meeting at Goldman's headquarters, I peppered Gary and Harvey with questions about the sustainability of first-quarter earnings. What business lines were operating above trend line? How much were they above trend line, and why? What business lines were operating below trend line? How much were they below trend line, and why? Management was reluctant to disclose much of the information I sought, but I did leave the meeting with the belief that the company's normal earnings power should be somewhere close to 15 percent of its tangible book value and that management was conservative and was bent on underpromising and overdelivering. When meeting with managements, I often hear a company's "party line"—a line that dwells on the company's greatness and future prosperity and that ignores the company's weaknesses. In the case of Goldman, my gut feel was that Gary and Harvey were straight shooters and that their opinions largely could be trusted.

On June 2, during a presentation at Deutsche Bank, Gary Cohn said the following about the normality of the first-quarter earnings: "We saw an environment where our clients were a little bit more active. We do not think that this is the upside per se. We feel like we have got plenty of upside potential in our business model." Of course, these words were music to my ears.

The music then continued as Gary listed reasons why Goldman should prosper in the future:

> We are, in many ways, a technology firm, with about one quarter of our employees in our technology division. We have made a number of key technology investments that provide us with a unique competitive advantage.
>
> We have transformed our financial profile. We have restructured our expense space. We have created robust tools and processes to inform our capital allocation decisions. We have a strong position within each of our businesses and have sold or shut down businesses that are likely to be dilutive to returns going forward. We are

in an improving competitive position. And, we are well positioned
to capture the opportunities as the environment improves.

Over the summer, I asked several competitors whether Gary's words were credible or were "BS." The competitors responded that Gary was a salesman but that his optimism was well founded and that Goldman was a powerhouse.

The more I learned about Goldman Sachs, the more I was convinced that we had made an exciting investment. But I still monitored the company closely, particularly on guard for any external development that might derail our analysis and conclusions. Occasionally, a black swan adverse event does derail one or more of our investments. When this happens, we must be ready to unemotionally rethink the economics of continuing to hold the investments—and, if necessary, sell.

This happened in the fall of 2014. At the time, we owned large positions in three oil and gas service companies and a smaller position in a producer of oil and gas. During the summer of 2014, the price of crude oil still was being supported at a high level by the OPEC cartel, and particularly by Saudi Arabia. It was clear to us at the time that increased production of oil from North American shale fields and from Iraq was creating excess capacity in the world, but we believed that it was in Saudi Arabia's interest to reduce its production in order to eliminate the excess capacity and thus to maintain prices at a high level. But we were wrong. Evidently, the leaders of Saudi Arabia concluded that, instead of continually reducing their production to offset the increasing production elsewhere, it was advantageous to "nip it in the bud" and let prices fall to a level where drilling new higher-cost North American oil wells would become uneconomic and, as a consequence, North American oil production would stall or fall.

The price of crude oil, which was roughly $100 per barrel during the summer of 2014, started to decline in September. The decline continued in October, and by early November the price broke below $80. I then analyzed detailed estimates and projections of the supply and demand by geographic region and came to the conclusion that, unless production was curtailed by political or military unrest in unstable countries or unless production was curtailed by Saudi Arabia, the surplus of crude oil would continue to grow. I asked myself: if Saudi Arabia intended to maintain high price levels by curtailing production, why did the Saudis let the price of crude fall as low as $80? Most "experts" and the media were predicting that the OPEC cartel would hold and that prices would recover, but there is an old expression that one should not pay attention to the noise in the market, but rather to the price of the fish. And the price of the fish was telling me that the cartel might not be holding. My obvious concern was that the earnings and values of our oil-related holdings would deteriorate in a lower-oil-price environment. Oil and gas companies would have less funds and less incentive to drill new wells, and the value of oil reserves in the ground would decline. I then tried to estimate what the normal price for oil would be if the cartel did not hold. My conclusion was that the normal price would be somewhere in the range of $55 to $70 per barrel. If long-term prices were above $70, a sufficient number of shale oil and other higher cost wells would be economic that there would be excess production. But if longer-term prices were below $55, an insufficient number of wells would be economic to satisfy world demand. I then concluded that if the longer-term prices of crude were in the range of $55 to $70, our four oil-related holdings no longer would be sufficiently attractive. Because I lacked confidence that Saudi Arabia would reduce its production, on November 13, I started selling the holdings. On November 27, at a meeting in Vienna, OPEC officially declared that it was abandoning its policy of controlling production and prices. By early 2015, we no longer owned any oil- and gas-related investments.

In very late 2014, I had a long conversation with a portfolio manager who continued to be heavily invested in oil-producing companies. He told me that my supply-demand numbers were wrong because they underestimated future demand from emerging countries, especially China. He e-mailed me two projections by Wall Street security analysts that showed a tightening oil market in 2015. I had read many reports by

Wall Street analysts and industry consultants. Almost all seemed to agree that there would be a surplus of supply in 2015 unless the Saudis curtailed production. It seemed to me that the portfolio manager had purposefully sought out two minority opinions that happened to agree with his original analysis—and had ignored the vast majority of opinions. He had closed his mind to a probable new development. He was engaged in wishful thinking. I believe that it is important for investors to avoid seeking out information that reinforces their original analyses. Instead, investors must be prepared and willing to change their analyses and minds when presented with new developments that adversely alter the fundamentals of an industry or company. Good investors should have open minds and be flexible.

In mid-2015, I had breakfast with the same portfolio manager who was retaining his holdings in oil-producing companies. He had given up on his theory that the oil market would tighten soon, but he now had a new theory. He believed that the five very large integrated international oil companies[4] likely would be interested in acquiring U.S. oil producers because of the political stability of the United States and because of the opportunity to use horizontal drilling and multistage fracking to economically increase reserves and production in shale formations. He believed that one or more of his oil holdings would be acquired at a premium price by one of the five giant companies. After the breakfast, I went to my Bloomberg terminal and discovered that there were 28 medium-sized U.S. oil and gas producers that had a market value of $5 billion or more. One never knows where lightning will strike, so one never knows which of the 28 companies would be acquired by the 5 very large integrated companies, if any. Since I would not know which company might be acquired, I could even my bets by purchasing an equal-sized position in each of the 28 companies. If each of the 5 large integrated companies indeed purchased one of the 28 during the next 12 months, and if the acquisition price was at a 30 percent premium to the market price, then the basket of my 28 holdings would appreciate by about 5 percent, other things being equal. Greenhaven tries to achieve annual returns of 15 to

20 percent, so the prospect of acquisitions adding 5 percent to a portion of our portfolio is not very exciting. And the 5 percent assumes that each of the 5 large companies is in the mood to make an acquisition during the next 12 months, which strikes me as a low-probability occurrence. Simply, the economics of the portfolio manager's new theory did not seem to justify an investment in the 28 companies. It seems to me that he was groping for a reason to continue holding his oil-producing companies. We have a straightforward approach. When we are wrong or when fundamentals turn against us, we readily admit we are wrong and we reverse our course. We do not seek new theories that will justify our original decision. We do not let errors fester and consume our attention. We sell and move on.

In late October 2015, a client, Mike Overlock, called to schedule a lunch date. Mike had been a star at Goldman Sachs, becoming a partner in 1982, head of the Mergers and Acquisitions Department in 1984, and co-head of the entire Investment Banking Department in 1990. In addition, in 1990, he was appointed to Goldman's Management Committee, which is the committee that largely managed the firm when it was a partnership. When Mike retired from Goldman, the *Wall Street Journal* called him "one of Wall Street's most powerful merger dealmakers." Mike, of course, knew that I had purchased shares of Goldman Sachs for his account, and I thought the subject of Goldman likely would come up at our lunch. So I decided to be prepared—very prepared in view of Mike's knowledge of the firm. I took out my file on Goldman, reviewed all my notes and memos, and rethought my rationale for purchasing the shares. And the more I rethought, the more I became convinced and excited about the probable rewards of owning the shares. I was happy. But I am almost always happy when working as an investment manager. What a perfect job, spending my days studying the world, economies, industries, and companies; thinking creatively; interviewing CEOs of companies; and having lunch with the Mike Overlocks. How lucky I am. How very, very lucky.

NOTES

1. Once a quarter, investment managers must disclose their holdings on an SEC Form 13-F.

2. The tangible book value is the shareholders' common equity less any goodwill or intangibles.

3. My logic behind the 10 percent is as follows:

   With respect to trading, by all reputation, Goldman generally has better and more profitable operations than the majority of its competitors. If Goldman did not earn a return of about 10 percent on its trading business, many of its competitors would not earn sufficient returns on some of their trading lines to warrant continuing the lines. As competitors exited their lower return lines, competition would decline, spreads would widen, and Goldman's returns would gravitate toward 10 percent.

   With respect to investing, Goldman mainly owns equities and loans. Over time, investors in common stocks have earned an average annual return of 9 to 10 percent. And over time, banks have earned more than 10 percent average annual return on their loan portfolios, assuming that the portfolios are normally leveraged with deposits and borrowings. Therefore, it is reasonable to conclude that Goldman's investing operations should see at least a 10 percent return on invested capital.

4. The five are BP, Chevron, Exxon, Royal Dutch, and Total.

14

A LETTER TO JACK ELGART

In 2008, a younger investment manager asked me to explain our approach to investing and to give him any additional advice that might be useful. In response to his request, I wrote the following letter.

• • •

Dear Jack,

Thank you for your questions, which I will try to answer in this letter. I apologize for the length of the letter. It is difficult to do justice to a complex subject in a few paragraphs. Also, please be mindful that there is nothing sacred about the way I invest or about my ideas. As in so many things in life, there are many differing approaches to being a successful investor.

There is a saying that going to church does not make you a Christian any more than standing in a garage makes you a car. And it also is true that having specific strategies and approaches to investing does not make you a Warren Buffett. But it helps, and it has helped me to make reasoned investment decisions, especially during difficult times.

Our central strategy is to purchase deeply undervalued securities of strong and growing companies that likely will appreciate sharply as the result of positive developments. Our reasoning is that the undervaluation, growth, and strength should provide protection against permanent loss, while the undervaluation, growth, strength, and positive developments should present the opportunity to earn high returns.

I emphasize that our first goal is to control the risks of permanent loss. When we analyze a security, we first look for the attributes that will protect us against incurring a loss that cannot be recovered within a reasonable period of time. We will not commence analyzing the positive attributes of a security until we are convinced that the risks of permanent loss in the security are relatively low.

Our emphasis on controlling risks leads us to be value investors as opposed to growth-stock investors. We have observed that, over the years, many growth stocks have permanently lost value due to a slow-down in their growth rates, often caused by maturing markets or by increased competition (including competition from new destructive technologies—Kodak being just one example).

Over the past 50+ years, the stock market has provided annual average returns of 9 to 10 percent (appreciation plus dividends). If an investor purchases a portfolio of undervalued stocks and if the stocks merely perform in line with the market, the investor's longer-term returns should average 9 to 10 percent. However, if the investor can find undervalued securities and can creatively project the occurrence of positive developments that already have not been discounted into the price of the securities, he can hope to earn outsized returns. Examples of positive developments include a cyclical upturn in the earnings of a company or industry, the solving of a problem that has been a drain of earnings, the introduction of an exciting new product or service, or the replacement of a weak management with a strong one. It sometimes takes a long time for a particular security to benefit from a positive development and to appreciate sharply. One has to be patient. But what happens if a predicted positive development fails to occur at all, which does happen? Then, the average stock still should provide average returns of 9 to 10 percent over time. This is not an unfavorable outcome. We are deprived of the icing, but we still get the cake.

Thus, in my opinion, an analytical, creative, and disciplined investor who uses sage judgment can achieve returns materially in excess of the market average. If such an investor succeeds in achieving average returns materially in excess of 9 to 10 percent, he eventually can become very wealthy through the power of compounding. *Compounding* is one of my favorite words. Compounding is powerful. Warren Buffett did not become one of the wealthiest men in the world by suddenly striking gold in a single highly successful investment, but rather by compounding the value of Berkshire Hathaway at a 20 percent or so rate for 45 years. If an investor can achieve an average annual return of 20 percent, then, after 45 years, an initial investment of $1 million will appreciate to $3.6 billion.[1] Wow!

However, while value investing sounds easy, one should remember that there are thousands of other investors trying to successfully do what you are trying to do, so value investing is a competitive (but fun and exciting) battle. To be a successful value investor, it helps to have a highly creative mind that is able to develop theses about the future, particularly about likely positive developments. I have given considerable thought to how an individual can increase his creativity, but the human mind is amorphous, and understanding the creative workings of the mind is like trying to get one's hands around a cloud. However, I would say that it is helpful to let your mind wander, to be open to new ideas and change, and to free your mind from preconceived notions. Creative ideas rarely come in a flash, but rather usually from a combination or a reinterpretation of existing ideas.

Value investors also need experience. After graduating from a business school and after a few years working as an investment professional, an intelligent and diligent investor likely will become proficient at playing the notes, but it still can require several additional years before he can play the music. As in music and sports, the best professionals tend to develop a rhythm and feel that comes with long practice and that leads to optimum results. In my opinion, the intuitive feel (or sixth sense) that most good investors develop partially comes from an innate ability and partially from experience.

In addition to creativity and experience, a good value investor needs the self-confidence to be able to make decisions that are counter to the combined conventional wisdom of other investors. The price of a stock at any one moment reflects the conventional wisdom of the market. Conceptually, a stock that appears out of favor and materially undervalued to you does not appear undervalued to most other investors. Otherwise, a sufficient number of other investors already would have decided to purchase the stock, driving its price to its intrinsic value. Therefore, a good value investor must make decisions based on his own analysis and judgment and must ignore the mass of opinions from Wall Street analysts, newspaper journalists, TV commentators, and others. He must be a contrarian, and he must be willing and able to feel lonely and uncomfortable. When purchasing a stock, it is usually better to feel uncomfortable than comfortable.

Also, decisions seldom are clear. There always are uncertainties about the fundamentals of a company, and every company has present or potential problems as well as present or future strengths. However, an investor can try to assess the probabilities of certain outcomes occurring and then make his decisions based on the probabilities. Investing is probabilistic.

To successfully assess probabilities and make good investment decisions, an investor should hold considerable amounts of information about the companies and industries he is investing in. Having superior information (both quantity and quality) can give an investor a competitive edge. To obtain information, we spend a large percentage of our time researching the fundamentals of companies.

While investing is not formularistic, there do seem to be a number of reoccurring patterns and strategies that one should take advantage of or should guard against:

1. Be careful not to let your mind acclimate to a present circumstance, and then lose perspective. This is particularly true after a long period of prosperity. During "bull" markets, many

investors tend to give themselves too much credit for favorable results and to give insufficient credit to the positive environment that played a large role in creating the results. This can lead to overconfidence on the part of the investor and resulting misassessments of risks.

2. Beware of projecting past or present trends into the future. The past often is an unreliable guide to the future. Steering an automobile by looking in the rearview mirror works as long as the road is straight, but is disaster when the road reaches a sharp curve. The same is true in investing.

3. Beware of seeking out information that reinforces your existing points of view or of screening out information that threatens to expose flaws in your existing beliefs. When you own a security, you are prone to be more accepting of good news about the security than bad news, and this can create a bias that leads to faulty decision making.

4. Intensively research stocks and industries, and pay attention to the quality of the information as well as the quantity. Quality information reduces uncertainty and risk. However, while it is dangerous to make decisions based on only a small amount of information, one should not miss investment opportunities due to overresearching an idea. You do not have to drink a whole bowl of soup to know how it tastes.

5. Be wary about basing investment decisions on predictions about the economy, interest rates, or stock market. There are so many variables that affect the direction of the economy, interest rates, or stock market that it is nearly impossible to identify, analyze, and weigh all the relevant variables, and even if this could be done, an investor would have difficulty estimating how much of the future already has been discounted into the price of individual securities. Experience has shown that investors are prone to overestimate how much they understand about the world, and underestimate the role of chance in events. Woody Allen once

said: "I am astounded by people who want to know the universe when it is hard enough to know your way around Chinatown."

6. Managements of companies possess more information about their companies than you ever will be able to possess. Pay more attention to what managements do than to what they say. Remember, managements, like most other people, tend to act in their self-interest. It often is a favorable sign when managements purchase shares of their companies for their own accounts, and vice versa. Favor managements who are highly incentivized to achieve higher prices for their shares.

7. Be particularly wary of projections made by managements and others who have vested interests in having their projections believed and acted upon.

8. Be wary of companies that largely have been "put together" through recent acquisitions. Normally, acquisitions are made through an auction process, with the acquiring company agreeing to pay the highest price. I agree with Warren Buffett that the smartest side to take in a bidding war is the losing side. After purchasing a painting at auction at Christie's or Sotheby's, I often am congratulated by my neighbors in the audience. My reaction is: why should anybody be congratulated for paying a price that no one else was willing to pay? When I value a company that has been acquisitive, I estimate that the parts of the businesses that recently were acquired are worth the price they were acquired at, plus some premium for subsequent growth or synergies, less a discount if I believe that the acquiring company overpaid. Thus, companies that largely have been put together in recent years normally are not worth a large premium to their stated book values.

9. Be aware of the laws of supply and demand. The balance between supply and demand normally is the main determinant of the market price of the item. Also, be aware that countervailing forces usually affect supply and demand. For example, when

an item is selling at a high price because of a tight supply, the market tightness often is mitigated or erased by new supplies (attracted by the high prices), reduced demand (motivated by the high prices), or substitution into less expensive items.

10. Be wary of stock recommendations made by others, especially by those in the media who may sound articulate and authoritative, but who lack the resources to be successful professional investors. A horse that can count to 10 is a wonderful horse, but not a wonderful mathematician.

11. Do not be overly influenced by the media. Because bad news sells, the media has a pessimistic bias. Over many years, a large percentage of the severe problems predicted by the media never materialized, or proved to be far less severe than predicted. The cover story of the August 13, 1979, issue of *Business Week* was titled "The Death of Equities." The article's gist was that investors were switching out of common stocks in favor of higher-yielding investments—and that it was likely that the stock market would not recover soon from the doldrums it had been in for many years. At the time the article was written, the S&P 500 Index was no higher than it had been 11 years earlier. Well, *Business Week* was dead wrong. Soon after the publication of the article, the stock market entered a strong bull market. Between August 1979 and August 2000, the S&P 500 Index increased from about 100 to about 1,500. An investor who purchased an S&P 500 Index fund in August 1979 and sold the fund 21 years later, would have enjoyed a 16 percent average annual return on his investment (including dividends).

12. Avoid over-relying on numbers and models. Investors often feel comfortable with numbers and models because they appear definitive. However, they can be misleading because they often are based on historical data that may not be repeatable or are based on assumptions that may not prove valid. We need numbers and models, but their utility should be paired with judgment and

common sense. There is the story of a statistician who drowned crossing a river that was only three feet deep on average. He obviously lacked both judgment and common sense.

13. Separate your analysis from your emotions. Especially during a difficult period, many investors become distraught, let their emotions dictate their investment decisions, and make decisions that are irrational and costly. By understanding your emotions and by understanding the nature of a difficult period, an investor can hope to organize and control his mind to think and act rationally.

14. Seek simplicity. An investor cannot be sure how an investment is going to turn out, but he can attempt to identify and analyze the key possibilities, then assess the odds of each possibility taking place, and finally make a reasoned decision based on the odds and estimated economics of the key possibilities. We live in a world of possibilities and probabilities, not certainties. It is logical that an investor can increase his chances of success if he can reduce the number of unknowns that he has to weigh. Thus, we are more confident when the outcomes of our investments are dependent on relatively few possibilities—few moving parts.

15. Realize that the trees do not grow to the heavens. Be cautious when the price of a security, or the market as a whole, sells at an inflated value relative to its historical norm. A material overvaluation can be dangerous, especially if it becomes accepted as a "new norm." If there is an adverse change in sentiment, an overvaluation can correct swiftly and markedly.

16. A number of years ago, I adopted a methodology that is useful in determining whether the stock market is overvalued. I started by analyzing the "earnings" of the S&P 500 Index for the 40-year period 1960 to 2000. My conclusions (reached with the help of regression analysis) were that the earnings have grown at about a 6.8 percent compound annual growth rate (CAGR) and that the trend-line (i.e., normal) earnings on the S&P 500 in 2000

should have been about 46.75. I then calculated that, during the same 40-year period, the S&P 500 Index "sold" at an average price-to-earnings (PE) ratio of 15.8 times, which, I reasoned, is the normal PE ratio for the stock market. Thus, based on these historical metrics, I concluded that the normal level of the S&P 500 Index in 2000 should have been about 739 (46.75 × 15.8). Since earnings have grown at a 6.8 percent CAGR and since I know of no reason why this level of growth should not continue, I can then project future normal values for the S&P 500. In 2010, for example, the normal value of the S&P 500 should be about 1,427 (739 incremented at a 6.8 percent rate for 10 years). Thus, in 2010, if the S&P 500 happens to sell at 1,725, I would conclude that, based on historic metrics, the stock market is overvalued by roughly 21 percent. Because we wish to buy low and sell high, knowledge of where the market is selling relative to its historical metrics often is helpful, especially when the market is selling at an inflated level.

17. Conceptually, any investor can attempt to increase his[2] returns by accepting additional risks. Treasury bills are considered risk free but pay low interest rates. Investment-grade corporate bonds are riskier but pay higher interest rates than Treasury bills. "Junk bonds" generally are quite risky but normally pay quite high interest rates. Similarly, some common stocks are riskier than others. Every investor must analyze risks of permanent loss and must decide how much risk he is willing to assume. There is no correct answer to the proper level of risk avoidance. It depends on the nature of the investment and on the needs, desires, and personality of the investor.

18. While an investor should work hard to avoid permanent loss, he must guard against being so risk averse that he turns down too many promising opportunities for fear of making a mistake. Even the best investors occasionally will err. To err is human— and we should not let errors dull our confidence or spirits.

19. Be prepared and willing to change your mind if your initial decision was flawed or if circumstances change. Be readily willing to admit that you made a mistake.

20. Invest for the longer term (two years at a minimum) and deemphasize the significance of short-term results. Most hedge funds and mutual funds and many other investors are under pressure to achieve short-term performance. Thus, there is fierce competition for ideas that will appreciate sharply over the next quarter or so. There is much less competition for stocks that have less certain shorter-term prospects, even if they appear to have excellent intermediate-term prospects—and that is where we normally want to be.

21. Do not attempt to "time" the stock market. The near-term direction of the stock market is determined by so many forces that it is difficult for anybody to identify all the relevant ones, let alone understand and weigh them and then determine the extent that they already are discounted into the market. Furthermore, the forces are dynamic, leaving market timers at the mercy of future developments that are difficult (and many times impossible) to predict. For all these reasons, most market timers do not seem to enjoy acceptable batting averages. We agree with Warren Buffett, who, at the 1994 Annual Meeting of Berkshire Hathaway, said: "I never have an opinion on the market because it would not be any good and it might interfere with opinions that are good."

22. Try to remain relatively fully invested as long as you can find a sufficient number of attractive securities. Because corporate earnings and the stock markets appreciate over time, if you are fully invested, you are swimming with the tide. However, when you cannot find a sufficient number of attractive securities to remain fully invested, be willing to hold cash. Do not stretch to remain fully invested. Further, if you perceive that there are excesses or other unacceptable risks in the economy, be willing to tighten your investment standards and sell stocks that had

acceptable risk profiles in a lower-risk economy but unacceptable risk profiles in a higher-risk economy.

23. Try to generally think and act positively and optimistically. Because over the longer run the stock market appreciates at a mid-single-digit annual rate, it normally is advantageous to have an optimistic view of the world rather than a pessimistic one.

24. Structure a concentrated portfolio, yet a diverse portfolio. Conceptually, the first stock one selects for a portfolio has the most favorable risk-to-reward ratio, and each succeeding selected stock has a somewhat less favorable risk-to-reward ratio. Thus, a concentrated portfolio of 15 to 25 stocks should provide materially better risk-adjusted returns than a portfolio of 30 to 50 stocks. Yet one should seek sufficient diversity that a few permanent losses do not permanently impair the value of the portfolio or the confidence of the portfolio manager. It is important for a portfolio manager to sleep well at night. To achieve both concentration and diversity, a portfolio might consist of 15 to 25 holdings, with no individual security accounting for more than 12 percent of the value of the portfolio and no one industry accounting for more than 25 percent. The limits should be based on costs, not on market value, so that the portfolio manager is not forced to sell shares in a holding that has appreciated sharply, but that still remains attractive.

25. Be relaxed and invest with a passion.

Investing is exciting and intellectually challenging. It is fun. It also can be highly profitable, especially for someone like you who is bright and highly motivated. I hope that if you are a successful investor and if you become wealthy, you will use your wealth wisely. I believe that Pericles (who was an Athenian general and leader in the fifth century before Christ) had it right when he stated in his Funeral Oration: "Wealth to us is not mere material for vainglory, but rather an opportunity for achievement." And Warren Buffett and Bill Gates have it right when they donate a large percentage of their wealth to charity—to help others who are far less fortunate in life than they.

I hope this letter is useful. Again, there are many approaches to investing successfully—many ways to skin a cat.

Best of luck with your investment career,

Ed Wachenheim

NOTES

1. For purposes of this calculation, I have omitted consideration of taxes on realized capital gains and on dividends, which, of course, in real life you cannot do.
2. In this letter, every time I refer to "he" or "his," I am also referring to "she" or "her."

ABOUT THE AUTHOR

Edgar Wachenheim III is chairman and CEO of Greenhaven Associates, an investment management firm he founded in 1987. He is a trustee of the Museum of Modern Art and the New York Public Library, where he chairs the Investment Committee. He has been a director of a number of corporations and currently is vice chairman of the board of Central National–Gottesman Corporation, a worldwide marketer and distributor of pulp and paper. Wachenheim is a graduate of Williams College and Harvard Business School, where he was elected a Baker Scholar after his first year of study. He lives in Rye, New York, with his wife in a home that it frequented by his four grown children and six grandchildren.

INDEX